Fodor's 98 Pocket New York City

D0827108

Reprinted from *Fodor's New York City '98*

Fodor's Travel Publications, Inc.
New York • Toronto • London • Sydney • Auckland
www.fodors.com/

Fodor's Pocket New York City

EDITORS: David Low, Audra Epstein

Editorial Contributors: Robert Andrews, Hannah Borgeson, David Brown, Matthew Lore, Amy McConnell, Anastasia Mills, Margaret Mittelbach, Jennifer Paull, Heidi Sarna, Helayne Schiff, M. T. Schwartzman, Dinah Spritzer, J. Walman, Stephen Wolf

Editorial Production: Janet Foley

Maps: David Lindroth, *cartographer*; Steven K. Amsterdam, *map editor*

Design: Fabrizio La Rocca, *creative director*; Lyndell Brookhouse-Gil, *cover design*; Jolie Novak, *photo editor*

Production/Manufacturing: Mike Costa

Cover Photograph: Catherine Karnow

Copyright

Special Sales

CONTENTS

Maps

ON THE ROAD WITH FODOR'S

WE'RE ALWAYS thrilled to get letters from readers, especially one like this:

It took us an hour to decide what book to buy and we now know we picked the best one. Your book was wonderful, easy to follow, very accurate, and good on pointing out eating places, informal as well as formal. When we saw other people using your book, we would look at each other and smile.

Our editors and writers are deeply committed to making every Fodor's guide "the best one"— not only accurate but always charming, brimming with sound recommendations and solid ideas, right on the mark in describing restaurants and hotels, and full of fascinating facts that make you view what you've traveled to see in a rich new light.

About Our Writers

Our success in achieving our goals—and in helping to make your trip the best of all possible vacations—is a credit to the hard work of our extraordinary writers.

David Low, a native New Yorker (born in Queens), revised the Arts chapter and the Greenwich Village, SoHo, and Little Italy and Chinatown exploring sections. He has had an obsessive interest in theater, movies, and other performing arts in the city since he saw his first Broadway play, *Baker Street*.

Editor and freelance writer **Hannah Borgeson** enjoys walking tours of Manhattan neighborhoods and reading about and visiting interesting architectural sites throughout the city, all of which helped her in updating portions of the Exploring Manhattan chapter.

Brooklyn updater **Matthew Lore** has lived in Park Slope for three years. "It's great once you get there," he loves to tell Manhattanites who think Brooklyn is just too far away.

Fodor's editor **Amy McConnell,** who worked on the chapters on Lodging and Exploring, has spent many a night evaluating the softness of mattresses and the deepness of bathtubs in New York City's swankiest hotels.

Anastasia Mills, Fodor's editor and the Nightlife updater, has taken full advantage of New York City's clubs and bars since the early '80s.

Freelance writer **Margaret Mittelbach** is a Los Angeles native who has lived in New York for the past nine years. She updated the information on exploring New York City with children.

Shopping updater (and Fodor's editorial staff member) **Jennifer Paull** would like to thank her family for her exasperating consumer profile.

Syndicated travel, food, and wine journalist **J. Walman,** who wrote the Dining chapter, dispenses culinary advice to the 2 million listeners of WEVD-AM.

Fodor's editor **Stephen Wolf,** who updated a few lower- and upper-Manhattan sections of this guide, always has an eye out for that perfect New York moment.

New This Year

We're proud to announce that the American Society of Travel Agents has endorsed Fodor's as its guidebook of choice. ASTA is the world's largest and most influential travel trade association, operating in more than 170 countries, with 27,000 members pledged to adhere to a strict code of ethics reflecting the Society's motto, "Integrity in Travel." ASTA shares Fodor's devotion to providing smart, honest travel information and advice to travelers, and we've long recommended that our readers consult ASTA member agents for the experience and professionalism they bring to the table.

On the Web, check out Fodor's site (www.fodors.com/) for information on major destinations around the world and travel-savvy interactive features. The Web site also lists the 80-plus radio stations nationwide that carry the Fodor's Travel Show, a live call-in program that airs every weekend. Tune in to hear guests discuss their wonderful adventures—or call in to get answers for your most pressing travel questions.

How to Use This Book

Organization

Up front is **Essential Information.** Under each listing you'll find tips and information that will help you accomplish what you need to in New York City. You'll also find addresses and telephone numbers of organizations and companies that offer destination-related services and detailed information and publications.

The first chapter in the guide, Destination: New York City, helps get you in the mood for your trip. The Exploring chapter is subdivided by neighborhood; each subsection recommends neighborhood sights and lists them alphabetically. The remaining chapters are arranged in alphabetical order by subject (dining, lodging, nightlife and the arts, and shopping).

Icons and Symbols

★　Our special recommendations

✕　Restaurant

🏠　Lodging establishment

☝　Good for kids (rubber duckie)

☞　Sends you to another section of the guide for more information

✉　Address

☎　Telephone number

☉　Opening and closing times

🎫　Admission prices (those we give apply to adults; substantially reduced fees are almost always available for children, students, and senior citizens)

Numbers in black circles that appear on the maps and in the margins correspond to one another.

Credit Cards

The following abbreviations are used: **AE,** American Express; **D,** Discover; **DC,** Diners Club; **MC,** MasterCard; and **V,** Visa.

Please Write to Us

You can use this book in the confidence that all prices and opening times are based on information supplied to us at press time; Fodor's cannot accept responsibility for any errors. Time inevitably brings changes, so always confirm information when it matters—especially if you're making a detour to visit a specific place. In addition, when making reservations be sure to mention if you have a disability or are traveling with children, if you prefer a private bath or a certain type of bed, or if you have specific dietary needs or other concerns.

Were the restaurants we recommended as described? Did our hotel picks exceed your expectations? Did you find a museum we recommended a waste of time? If you have complaints, we'll look into them and revise our entries when the facts warrant it. If you've discovered a special place that we haven't included, we'll pass the information along to our correspondents and have them check it out. So send us your feedback, positive *and* negative: e-mail us at editors@fodors.com (specifying the name of the book on the subject line) or write the New York City editor at Fodor's, 201 East 50th Street, New York, New York 10022. Have a wonderful trip!

Karen Cure

Editorial Director

Manhattan Neighborhoods

Manhattan Subways

Subway Lines

▬▬▬▬▬	BMT
═════	IND
▪▪▪▪▪	IRT

Essential
Information

SMART TRAVEL TIPS

Basic Information on Traveling in New York City, Savvy Tips to Make Your Trip a Breeze, and Companies and Organizations to Contact

AIR TRAVEL

MAJOR AIRLINE OR LOW-COST CARRIER?

Most people choose a flight based on price. Yet there are other issues to consider. Major airlines offer the greatest number of departures; smaller airlines—including regional, low-cost and no-frill airlines—usually have a more limited number of flights daily. Major airlines have frequent-flyer partners, which allow you to credit mileage earned on one airline to your account with another. Low-cost airlines offer a definite price advantage and fewer restrictions, such as advance-purchase requirements. Safety-wise, low-cost carriers as a group have a good history, but **check the safety record before booking** any low-cost carrier; call the Federal Aviation Administration's Consumer Hotline (☞ Complain If Necessary, *below*).

➤MAJOR AIRLINES: **America West** (☎ 800/235–9292). **American** (☎ 800/433–7300). **Continental** (☎ 800/525–0280). **Delta** (☎ 800/221–1212). **Northwest** (☎ 800/225–2525). **TWA** (☎ 800/221–2000). **United**

(☎ 800/241–6522). **US Airways** (☎ 800/428–4322).

➤LOW-COST CARRIERS: **Kiwi International** (☎ 800/538–5494). **Midway** (☎ 800/446–4392). **Tower Air** (☎ 718/553–8500).

➤FROM THE U.K.: **Air India** (☎ 0181/745–1000). **American** (☎ 0345/789–789). **British Airways** (☎ 0345/222–111). **El Al** (☎ 0171/957–4100). **Kuwait Airways** (☎ 0171/412–0007). **United** (☎ 0800/888–555). **Virgin Atlantic** (☎ 01293/747–747). **Continental** (☎ 0800/776–464) and BA depart from Gatwick and Manchester, and Continental also operates from Birmingham.

GET THE LOWEST FARE

The least-expensive airfares to New York are priced for round-trip travel. Major airlines usually require that you **book in advance and buy the ticket within 24 hours,** and you may have to **stay over a Saturday night.** It's smart to **call a number of airlines, and when you are quoted a good price, book it on the spot**—the same fare may not be available on the same flight the next day. Airlines generally allow you to change your return date for a fee of $25–$50. If you don't use your ticket you can apply the cost toward the purchase of a new ticket, again for a small charge. However, most low-fare tickets are nonrefundable. To get the lowest airfare, **check different routings.** If your destination or home city has more than one gateway, compare prices to and from different airports. Also price off-peak flights, which may be significantly less expensive.

To save money on flights from the United States and back, **look into an APEX or Super-PEX ticket.** APEX tickets must be booked in advance and have certain restrictions. Super-PEX tickets, when available, can be purchased at the airport on the day of departure.

DON'T STOP UNLESS YOU MUST

When you book, **look for nonstop flights** and **remember that "direct" flights stop at least once.** Try to **avoid connecting flights,** which require a change of plane. Ask if your airline operates every segment of a connecting flight—you may find that your preferred carrier flies you only part of the way.

USE AN AGENT

Travel agents, especially those who specialize in finding the lowest fares (☞ Discounts & Deals, *below*), can be especially helpful when booking a plane ticket. When you're quoted a price, **ask your agent if the price is likely to**

get any lower. Good agents know the seasonal fluctuations of airfares and can usually anticipate a sale or fare war. However, waiting can be risky: The fare could go *up* as seats become scarce, and you may wait so long that your preferred flight sells out. A wait-and-see strategy works best if your plans are flexible, but if you must arrive and depart on certain dates, don't delay.

AVOID GETTING BUMPED

Airlines routinely overbook planes, knowing that not everyone with a ticket will show up, but sometimes everyone does. When that happens, airlines ask for volunteers to give up their seats. In return these volunteers usually get a certificate for a free flight and are rebooked on the next flight out. If there are not enough volunteers the airline must choose who will be denied boarding. The first to get bumped are passengers who checked in late and those flying on discounted tickets, **so get to the gate and check in as early as possible,** especially during peak periods.

Always **bring a photo ID to the airport.** You may be asked to show it before you can check in.

ENJOY THE FLIGHT

For better service, **fly smaller or regional carriers,** which often have higher passenger-satisfaction ratings. Sometimes you'll find leather seats, more legroom, and better food. For more legroom, **request** an emergency-aisle seat; don't however, sit in the row in front of the emergency aisle or in front of a bulkhead, where seats may not recline. If you don't like airline food, **ask for special meals when booking.** These can be vegetarian, low-cholesterol, or kosher, for example. To avoid jet lag, try to maintain a normal routine while traveling. At night **get some sleep.** By day **eat light meals, drink water, and move about the cabin** to stretch your legs.

COMPLAIN IF NECESSARY

If your baggage goes astray or your flight goes awry, complain right away. Most carriers require that you file a claim immediately.

➤AIRLINE COMPLAINTS: U.S. Department of Transportation Aviation Consumer Protection Division (✉ C-75, Washington, DC 20590, ☎ 202/366–2220). Federal Aviation Administration (FAA) Consumer Hotline (☎ 800/322–7873).

AIRPORTS & TRANSFERS

The major airports are **La Guardia Airport** and **JFK International Airport,** both in the borough of Queens, and **Newark International Airport** in New Jersey.

Flying time is 1½ hours from Chicago, five hours from Los Angeles, and eight hours from London.

➤AIRPORT INFORMATION: La Guardia Airport (☎ 718/533–3400). JFK International Airport (☎ 718/244–4444). Newark International Airport (☎ 201/961–6000).

TRANSFERS

➤LA GUARDIA AIRPORT: Taxis cost $17–$29 plus tolls (which may be as high as $4) and take 20–40 minutes. Group fares run $9–$10 per person (plus a share of tolls).

Carey Airport Express (☎ 718/632–0500) buses depart for Manhattan every 20–30 minutes from 6:45 AM to midnight, from all terminals. It's a 40-minute ride to 42nd Street and Park Avenue, directly opposite Grand Central Terminal. The bus continues from there to the Port Authority Bus Terminal, and then to several major midtown hotels. The bus fare is $10; pay the driver. The **Gray Line Airport Shuttle Minibus** (☎ 212/315–3006 or 800/451–0455) serves major Manhattan hotels and Port Authority directly to and from the airport. The fare is $13.50 per person; make arrangements at the ground transportation center or use the courtesy phone.

The most economical way to reach Manhattan is to ride Bus M-60 (there are no luggage facilities on this bus) to 116th Street and Broadway, across from Columbia University. From there, you can catch the Subway 1 or 9 to midtown. Alternatively, you can take Bus Q-33 to either the Roosevelt Avenue–Jackson Heights station, where you can catch Subway E or

F, or the 74th Street–Broadway station, where you can catch Subway 7. Allow 90 minutes for the entire trip to midtown; the total cost is $3. You can use exact change for your bus fare, but you will have to purchase a token or MetroCard to enter the subway.

➤JFK INTERNATIONAL AIRPORT: Taxis cost $30–$38 plus tolls (which may be as much as $4) and take 35–60 minutes.

Carey Airport Express buses depart for Manhattan every 20–30 minutes from 6 AM to midnight, from all JFK terminals. The ride to 42nd Street and Park Avenue (Grand Central Terminal) takes about one hour. The bus continues from there to the Port Authority Bus Terminal, and to several major midtown hotels. The bus fare is $13; pay the driver. The Gray Line Airport Shuttle Minibus serves major Manhattan hotels and Port Authority directly from the airport; the cost is $16.50 per person. Make arrangements at the airport's ground transportation counter or use the courtesy phone.

New York Helicopter offers private charter flights between the airport and one of four heliports in Manhattan. Helicopters leave from the General Aviation Terminal and set you down in the city 10 minutes later. The one-way fare is $299 for up to five people.

The cheapest but slowest means of getting to Manhattan is to take the

Port Authority's free shuttle bus, which stops at all terminals, to the Howard Beach subway station, where you can catch the A train into Manhattan. Alternatively, you can take Bus Q-10 (there are no luggage facilities on this bus) to the Union Turnpike–Kew Gardens station, where you can catch the Subway E or F. Or you can take Bus B-15 to New Lots station and catch Subway 3. Allow at least two hours for the trip; the total cost is $1.50 if you use the shuttle or $3 if you use the Q-10 or B-15. You can use exact change for your fare on the Q-10 and B-15, but you will need to purchase a token to enter the subway.

➤NEWARK AIRPORT: Taxis cost $34–$38 plus tolls ($10) and take 20–45 minutes. "Share and Save" group rates are available for up to four passengers between 8 AM and midnight; make arrangements with the airport's taxi dispatcher.

NJ Transit Airport Express (☎ 201/762–5100) buses depart for the Port Authority Bus Terminal, at 8th Avenue and 42nd Street, every 15 minutes on weekdays from 4:45 AM to 3:45 AM; on weekends, service runs nearly as frequently from 4:45 AM until 3 AM. From Port Authority, it's a short cab ride to midtown hotels. The ride takes 30–45 minutes. The fare is $7; buy your ticket inside the airport terminal.

Olympia Airport Express (☎ 212/964–6233 or 718/622–7700) buses leave for Grand Central Terminal and Penn Station about every 20 minutes, and 1 World Trade Center (WTC) about every 30 minutes, from around 6 AM to midnight. The trip takes roughly 45 minutes to Grand Central and Penn Station, 20 minutes to WTC. The fare is $7. At press time, a new route was planned between Port Authority and Newark. Buses will run every 20 minutes 5 AM–midnight. The fare is $10.

The Gray Line Airport Shuttle Minibus serves major Manhattan hotels and Port Authority directly to and from the airport. Passengers pay $14; make arrangements at the airport's ground transportation center or use the courtesy phone.

If you are arriving in Newark, you can take New Jersey Transit's Airlink buses, which leave every 20 minutes from 6:15 AM to 2 AM, to Penn Station in Newark. The ride takes about 20 minutes; the fare is $4. (Be sure to have exact change.) From there, you can catch one of the PATH trains, which run to Manhattan 24 hours a day. The trains depart every 10 minutes on weekdays, every 15–30 minutes on weeknights, and every 20–30 minutes on weekends, stopping at the WTC and at five stations along 6th Avenue—Christopher Street, 9th Street, 14th Street, 23rd Street, and 33rd Street. The fare is $1.

►CAR SERVICES: Car services are a great deal, because the driver will often meet you on the concourse or in the baggage-claim area and help you with your luggage. Call 24 hours in advance for reservations, or at least a half day before your flight's departure.

All State Car and Limousine Service (☎ 212/741–7440, FAX 212/727–2391). **Carey Limousines** (☎ 212/599–1122 or 800/336–4646). **Carmel Car and Limousine Service** (☎ 212/666–6666). **Dav-El Services** (☎ 212/645–4242 or 800/922–0343). **Eastside Limo Service** (☎ 212/744–9700, FAX 718/937–9400). **Greenwich Limousine** (☎ 212/868–4733 or 800/385–1033). **London Towncars** (☎ 212/988–9700 or 800/221–4009, FAX 718/786–7625). **Manhattan International Limo** (☎ 718/729–4200 or 800/221–7500, FAX 718/937–6157). **Sherwood Silver Bay Limousine Service** (☎ 718/472–0183 or 800/752–4540, FAX 718/361–5693). **Skyline** (☎ 212/741–3711 or 800/533–6325). **American Media Tours** (☎ 212/255–5908) provides car services exclusively for business accounts.

►BY HELICOPTER: For private charter helicopter service, contact **New York Helicopter** (☎ 800/645–3494, FAX 516/756–2694).

BUS TRAVEL

Bus lines feed into the **Port Authority Terminal** (☎ 212/564–8484). Individual bus lines serving New York include **Greyhound Lines** (☎ 212/971–6404 or 800/231–2222); **Adirondack, Pine Hill,** and **New York Trailways** (☎ 800/225–6815) from upstate New York; **Bonanza Bus Lines** (☎ 800/556–3815) from New England; **Martz Trailways** (☎ 800/233–8604) from Philadelphia and northeastern Pennsylvania; **New Jersey Transit** (☎ 201/762–5100) from around New Jersey; **Peter Pan Trailways** (☎ 413/781–2900 or 800/343–9999) from New England; and **Vermont Transit** (☎ 802/864–6811 or 800/451–3292) from New England.

The **George Washington Bridge Bus Station** (☎ 212/564–1114) is at Fort Washington Avenue and Broadway between 178th and 179th streets in Washington Heights. Six bus lines, serving northern New Jersey and Rockland County, New York, make daily stops there from 5 AM to 1 AM. The terminal connects with the 175th Street Station on Subway A, making it slightly more convenient for travelers going to and from the West Side.

WITHIN NEW YORK

Most buses follow easy-to-understand routes along the Manhattan grid. Routes go up or down the north–south avenues or east and west on the major two-way crosstown streets. Most bus routes operate 24 hours, but service is infrequent late at night. Traffic jams—a potential threat at any time or place in Manhattan—can make rides maddeningly slow. New bus stop signs were introduced in the fall of 1996 and should be in place throughout the city by 1998. Look for a light-blue sign (or green for an express bus) on a green pole; bus numbers and routes are listed, with the current stop's name underneath. Bus fare is the same as subway fare: $1.50 at press time, in coins (no change is given) or a subway token or MetroCard. When using a token or cash, you can ask the driver for a free transfer coupon, good for one change to an intersecting route. Legal transfer points are listed on the back of the slip. Transfers have time limits of at least two hours, often longer. You cannot use the transfer to enter the subway system. However, you can **transfer free from bus to subway or subway to bus with the MetroCard.** You must start with the MetroCard and use it again within two hours to complete your trip.

Route maps and schedules are posted at many bus stops in Manhattan and at major stops throughout the other boroughs. Each of the five boroughs of New York has a separate bus map;

they're available from some sub-way token booths. The best places to obtain them are the Convention and Visitors Bureau at Columbus Circle or the information kiosks in Grand Central Terminal and Penn Station.

➤ROUTE INFORMATION: The **MTA** (☎ 718/330–1234), open daily 6–9, has information about routes, bus stops, and hours of operation. There is also a status information hot line (☎ 718/243–7777), which is updated hourly between 6 and 9.

CAR RENTAL

Rates in New York City begin at $46 a day and $205 a week for an economy car with air-condition-ing, automatic transmission, and unlimited mileage. This does not include tax on car rentals, which is 13¼%.

➤MAJOR AGENCIES: **Avis** (☎ 800/331–1212; 800/879–2847 in Canada). **Budget** (☎ 800/527–0700; 0800/181181 in the U.K.). **Dollar** (☎ 800/800–4000; 0990/565656 in the U.K., where it is known as Eurodollar). **Hertz** (☎ 800/654–3131; 800/263–0600 in Canada; 0345/555888 in the U.K.). **National InterRent** (☎ 800/227–7368; 0345/222525 in the U.K., where it is known as Europcar InterRent).

CUT COSTS

To get the best deal, **book through a travel agent who is willing to shop around.** When pricing cars, **ask about the location of the rental lot.** Some off-airport loca-tions offer lower rates, and their lots are only minutes from the ter-minal via complimentary shuttle. You also may want to **price local car-rental companies,** whose rates may be lower still, although their service and maintenance may not be as good as those of a name-brand agency. Remember to ask about required deposits and can-cellation penalties.

Before you pick up a car in one city and leave it in another, **ask about drop-off charges or one-way service fees,** which can be substantial. Note, too, that some rental agencies charge extra if you return the car before the time specified on your contract.

Also **ask your travel agent about a company's customer-service record.** How has it responded to late plane arrivals and vehicle mishaps? Are there often lines at the rental counter, and, if you're traveling during a holiday period, does a confirmed reservation guar-antee you a car?

NEED INSURANCE?

When driving a rented car you are generally responsible for any dam-age to or loss of the vehicle. You also are liable for any property damage or personal injury that you may cause while driving. Be-fore you rent, **see what coverage you already have** under the terms of your personal auto-insurance policy and credit cards.

BEWARE SURCHARGES

To avoid a hefty refueling fee, **fill the tank just before you turn in the car,** but be aware that gas stations near the rental outlet may overcharge.

MEET THE REQUIREMENTS

In New York you must be 18 to rent a car, and rates may be higher if you're under 25. You'll pay extra for additional drivers (about $2 per day). Residents of the United Kingdom will need a reservation voucher, a passport, a U.K. driver's license, and a travel policy that covers each driver, in order to pick up a car.

CUSTOMS & DUTIES

ENTERING THE U.S.

Visitors age 21 and over may import the following into the United States: 200 cigarettes or 50 cigars or 2 kilograms of tobacco, 1 liter of alcohol, and gifts worth $100. Prohibited items include meat products, seeds, plants, and fruits.

ENTERING CANADA

If you've been out of Canada for at least seven days you may bring in C$500 worth of goods duty-free. If you've been away for fewer than seven days but more than 48 hours, the duty-free allowance drops to C$200; if your trip lasts 24–48 hours, the allowance is C$50. You may not pool allowances with family members.

Goods claimed under the C$500 exemption may follow you by mail; those claimed under the lesser exemptions must accompany you.

Alcohol and tobacco products may be included in the seven-day and 48-hour exemptions but not in the 24-hour exemption. If you meet the age requirements of the province or territory through which you reenter Canada you may bring in, duty-free, 1.14 liters (40 imperial ounces) of wine or liquor *or* 24 12-ounce cans or bottles of beer or ale. If you are 16 or older you may bring in, duty-free, 200 cigarettes and 50 cigars; these items must accompany you.

You may send an unlimited number of gifts worth up to C$60 each duty-free to Canada. Label the package UNSOLICITED GIFT—VALUE UNDER $60. Alcohol and tobacco are excluded.

➤INFORMATION: **Revenue Canada** (✉ 2265 St. Laurent Blvd. S, Ottawa, Ontario K1G 4K3, ☎ 613/993–0534; 800/461–9999 in Canada).

ENTERING THE U.K.

From countries outside the European Union, including the United States, you may import, duty-free, 200 cigarettes or 50 cigars; 1 liter of spirits or 2 liters of fortified or sparkling wine or liqueurs; 2 liters of still table wine; 60 milliliters of perfume; 250 milliliters of toilet water;

plus £136 worth of other goods, including gifts and souvenirs.

➤INFORMATION: **HM Customs and Excise** (✉ Dorset House, Stamford St., London SE1 9NG, ☎ 0171/202–4227).

DISCOUNTS & DEALS

DIAL FOR DOLLARS

To save money, **look into "1-800" discount reservations services,** which use their buying power to get a better price on hotels, airline tickets, even car rentals. When booking a room, always **call the hotel's local toll-free number** (if one is available) rather than the central reservations number— you'll often get a better price. Always ask about special packages or corporate rates.

➤AIRLINE TICKETS: ☎ 800/FLY–4–LESS. ☎ 800/FLY–ASAP.

➤HOTEL ROOMS: **Accommodations Express** (☎ 800/444–7666). **Central Reservation Service (CRS)** (☎ 800/548–3311). **Hotel Reservations Network (HRN)** (☎ 800/964–6835). **Quickbook** (☎ 800/789–9887). **Room Finders USA** (☎ 800/473–7829). **RMC Travel** (☎ 800/245–5738). **Steigenberger Reservation Service** (☎ 800/223–5652).

EMERGENCIES

Dial 911 for **police, fire,** or **ambulance** in an emergency (TTY is available for the hearing impaired).

➤DOCTOR: **Doctors on Call, 24-hour house-call service** (☎ 212/737–2333). Near midtown, 24-hour emergency rooms are open at **St. Luke's–Roosevelt Hospital** (✉ 59th St., between 9th and 10th Aves., ☎ 212/523–6800) and **St. Vincent's Hospital** (✉ 7th Ave. and 12th St., ☎ 212/604–7997).

➤DENTIST: The **Emergency Dental Service** (☎ 212/679–3966 or 212/679–4172 after 8 PM) will make a referral.

➤HOT LINES: **Victims' Services** (☎ 212/577–7777), **Mental Health** (☎ 212/219–5599 or 800/527–7474 for information after 5 PM), **Sex Crimes Report Line** (☎ 212/267–7273).

➤24-HOUR PHARMACY: **Kaufman's Pharmacy** (✉ Lexington Ave. and 50th St., ☎ 212/755–2266) is open around the clock, but its prices are exorbitant; **Genovese** (✉ 2nd Ave. at 68th St., ☎ 212/772–0104) is less expensive. Before 10 or 11 PM, look for a pharmacy in a neighborhood that keeps late hours, such as Greenwich Village or the Upper West Side, for better deals.

INSURANCE

Travel insurance is the best way to **protect yourself against financial loss.** The most useful policies are trip-cancellation-and-interruption, default, medical, and comprehensive insurance.

Without insurance you will lose all or most of your money if you cancel your trip, regardless of the reason. It's essential that you **buy trip-cancellation-and-interruption insurance,** particularly if your airline ticket, cruise, or package tour is nonrefundable and cannot be changed. When considering how much coverage you need, look for a policy that will cover the cost of your trip plus the nondiscounted price of a one-way airline ticket, should you need to return home early. Also **consider default or bankruptcy insurance,** which protects you against a supplier's failure to deliver.

Citizens of the United Kingdom can buy an annual travel-insurance policy valid for most vacations during the year in which it's purchased. According to the Association of British Insurers, a trade association representing 450 insurance companies, it's wise to buy extra medical coverage when you visit the United States.

Always **buy travel insurance directly from the insurance company**; if you buy it from a travel agency or tour operator that goes out of business you probably will not be covered for the agency or operator's default—a major risk. Before you make any purchase, **review your existing health and home-owner's policies** to find out whether they cover expenses incurred while traveling.

➤TRAVEL INSURERS: In the United States, **Access America** (✉ 6600 W. Broad St., Richmond, VA 23230, ☎ 804/285–3300 or 800/284–8300), **Carefree Travel Insurance** (✉ Box 9366, 100 Garden City Plaza, Garden City, NY 11530, ☎ 516/294–0220 or 800/323–3149), **Near Travel Services** (✉ Box 1339, Calumet City, IL 60409, ☎ 708/868–6700 or 800/654–6700), **Travel Guard International** (✉ 1145 Clark St., Stevens Point, WI 54481, ☎ 715/345–0505 or 800/826–1300), **Travel Insured International** (✉ Box 280568, East Hartford, CT 06128-0568, ☎ 860/528–7663 or 800/243–3174), **Travelex Insurance Services** (✉ 11717 Burt St., Suite 202, Omaha, NE 68154-1500, ☎ 402/445–8637 or 800/228–9792, FAX 800/867–9531), **Wallach & Company** (✉ 107 W. Federal St., Box 480, Middleburg, VA 20118, ☎ 540/687–3166 or 800/237–6615). In Canada, **Mutual of Omaha** (✉ Travel Division, 500 University Ave., Toronto, Ontario M5G 1V8, ☎ 416/598–4083; 800/268–8825 in Canada). In the United Kingdom, **Association of British Insurers** (✉ 51 Gresham St., London EC2V 7HQ, ☎ 0171/600–3333).

MONEY

ATMS

Before leaving home, **make sure that your credit cards have been programmed for ATM use.**

➤ATM LOCATIONS: **Cirrus**
(☎ 800/424–7787). **Plus**
(☎ 800/843–7587).

PASSPORTS & VISAS

CANADIANS

A passport is not required to enter
the United States.

U.K. CITIZENS

British citizens need a valid passport to enter the United States. If
you are staying for fewer than 90
days on vacation, with a return
or onward ticket, you probably
will not need a visa. However,
you will need to fill out the Visa
Waiver Form, 1-94W, supplied by
the airline.

➤INFORMATION: **London Passport
Office** (☎ 0990/21010) for fees
and documentation requirements
and to request an emergency pass-
port. **U.S. Embassy Visa Informa-
tion Line** (☎ 01891/200–290) for
U.S. visa information; calls cost
49p per minute. **U.S. Embassy
Visa Branch** (✉ 5 Upper
Grosvenor St., London W1A 2JB)
for U.S. visa information; send a
self-addressed, stamped envelope.
Write the **U.S. Consulate General**
(✉ Queen's House, Queen St.,
Belfast BTI 6EO) if you live in
Northern Ireland.

SAFETY

Despite New York's bad reputation in the area of crime, most
people live here for years without
being robbed or assaulted. Nevertheless, as in any large city, travelers make particularly easy marks
for pickpockets and hustlers, so **be
cautious.**

Do **ignore the panhandlers** on the
streets (some aggressive, many
homeless), people who offer to
hail you a cab (they often appear
at Penn Station, Port Authority,
and Grand Central Terminal), and
limousine and gypsy cab drivers
who offer you a ride. Someone
who appears to have had an acci-
dent at the exit door of a bus may
flee with your wallet or purse if
you attempt to give aid; the individual who approaches you with a
complicated story is probably
playing a confidence game and
hopes to get something from you.
Also **beware of strangers jostling
you in crowds** or someone tapping
your shoulder from behind.

Keep jewelry out of sight on the
street; better yet, **leave valuables
at home.** Don't wear gold chains
or gaudy jewelry, even if it's fake.
Women should **never hang a
purse on a chair in a restaurant** or
on a hook in a rest-room stall.
Men are advised to **carry wallets
in front pants pockets** rather than
in their hip or back pockets.
Many New Yorkers carry a "mug-
ging wallet"—a cheap wallet with
a small amount of money inside,
which you won't mind relinquish-
ing—just in case.

Avoid deserted blocks in out-of-
the-way neighborhoods. If you
end up in an empty area or a side

street that feels unsafe, it probably is. A brisk, purposeful pace helps deter trouble wherever you go.

Although the subway runs round the clock, it is usually safest during the day and early evening. Most residents of the city have a rough cut-off time—10 or 11 PM—past which they avoid riding the subway trains. The subway system is much safer than it once was, but to **err on the side of caution,** you may want to travel by bus or taxi after the theater or a concert. If you do take the subway at night, stick to crowds.

SUBWAYS

The 714-mi subway system operates 24 hours a day and, especially within Manhattan, serves most of the places you'll want to visit. It's cheaper than a cab and, during the workweek, often faster than either cabs or buses. Air-conditioned cars predominate on every line. Still, the New York subway is not problem-free. Many trains are crowded and noisy. Although trains usually run frequently, especially during rush hours, you never know when some incident somewhere on the line may stall traffic. Don't write off the subway—some 3.5 million passengers ride it every day without incident—but stay alert (☞ Safety, *above*).

Subway fares are $1.50. It is advisable to **buy several tokens at one time** to avoid having to wait in line later. However, for four or more subway trips, you might find it easier to use the MTA's new MetroCard Gold, a thin, plastic card with a magnetic strip; swipe it through the reader at the turnstile, and the cost of the fare is automatically deducted. Most major subway stations accept the cards, and all 469 stations are scheduled to accept MetroCard by the end of 1997. They are sold at all subway stations where they are accepted and at some stores—look for an AUTHORIZED SALES AGENT sign. You can buy a card for a minimum of $3 (2 trips) and a maximum of $80, in $6 increments. You can add more money to a card, and more than one person can use the same card: Swipe it through the turnstile once for each rider. Both tokens and MetroCards permit unlimited transfers.

Most subway entrances are located at street corners and are marked by lampposts with globe-shaped lights. Subway lines are named for numbers and letters, such as the 3 line or the A line. Some lines run "express" and skip lots of stops; others are "locals" and make all stops. Each station entrance has a sign indicating the lines that run through the station; some stations are also marked UPTOWN ONLY or DOWNTOWN ONLY. Before entering subway stations, **read the signs carefully**—one of the most frequent mistakes visitors make is taking the train in the wrong direction. Maps of the full subway system are posted on trains near the doors and at stations. You can usually pick up free maps at token booths, too.

For route information, **ask the token clerk or a transit police officer or a fellow rider.** Most New Yorkers are eager to be helpful.

➤ROUTE INFORMATION: The **MTA** (☎ 718/330–1234) daily 6–9.

TELEPHONES
Make sure that the pay phone is labeled as a NYNEX telephone; the unmarked variety are notorious change-eaters. There are also public credit card phones scattered around the city. If you want to consult a directory or make a more leisurely call, pay phones in the lobbies of office buildings or hotels (some of which take credit cards) are a better choice.

The area code for Manhattan is 212; for Brooklyn, Queens, the Bronx, and Staten Island, it's 718. Pay telephones cost 25¢ for the first three minutes of a local call (this includes calls between 212 and 718 area codes); an extra deposit is required for each additional minute.

CALLING HOME
AT&T, MCI, and Sprint long-distance services make calling home relatively convenient and let you avoid hotel surcharges. Typically you dial an 800 number in the United States.

➤TO OBTAIN ACCESS CODES: **AT&T USADirect** (☎ 800/874–4000). **MCI Call USA** (☎ 800/444–4444). **Sprint Express** (☎ 800/793–1153).

TOUR OPERATORS
Buying a prepackaged tour or independent vacation can make your trip to New York less expensive and more hassle-free. Because everything is prearranged you'll spend less time planning. Operators that handle several hundred thousand travelers per year can use their purchasing power to give you a good price. Their high volume may also indicate financial stability. But some small companies provide more personalized service; because they tend to specialize, they may also be more knowledgeable about a given area.

A GOOD DEAL?
The more your package or tour includes, the better you can predict the ultimate cost of your vacation. Find out what's covered, and **beware of hidden costs.** Are taxes, tips, and service charges included? Transfers and baggage handling? Entertainment and excursions? These can add up.

If the package or tour you are considering is priced lower than in your wildest dreams, **be skeptical.** Also, **make sure your travel agent knows the accommodations** and other services. Ask about the hotel's location, room size, beds, and whether it has a pool, room service, or programs for children, if you care about these. Has your agent been there in person or sent others you can contact?

BUYER BEWARE

Each year consumers are stranded or lose their money when tour operators—even very large ones with excellent reputations—go out of business. So **check out the operator.** Find out how long the company has been in business, and ask several agents about its reputation. **Don't book unless the firm has a consumer-protection program.**

Members of the National Tour Association and United States Tour Operators Association are required to set aside funds to cover your payments and travel arrangements in case the company defaults. Nonmembers may carry insurance instead. Look for the details, and for the name of an underwriter with a solid reputation, in the operator's brochure. Note: When it comes to tour operators, **don't trust escrow accounts.** Although the Department of Transportation watches over charter-flight operators, no regulatory body prevents tour operators from raiding the till. You may want to protect yourself by buying travel insurance that includes a tour-operator default provision.

It's also a good idea to choose a company that participates in the American Society of Travel Agents' Tour Operator Program

(TOP). This gives you a forum if there are any disputes between you and your tour operator; ASTA will act as mediator.

➤ TOUR-OPERATOR RECOMMENDATIONS: **National Tour Association** (✉ NTA, 546 E. Main St., Lexington, KY 40508, ☎ 606/226–4444 or 800/755–8687). **United States Tour Operators Association** (✉ USTOA, 342 Madison Ave., Suite 1522, New York, NY 10173, ☎ 212/599–6599, FAX 212/599–6744). **American Society of Travel Agents** (☞ Travel Agencies, *below*).

USING AN AGENT

Travel agents are excellent resources. In fact, large operators accept bookings made only through travel agents. But it's a good idea to **collect brochures from several agencies,** because some agents' suggestions may be influenced by relationships with tour and package firms that reward them for volume sales. If you have a special interest, **find an agent with expertise in that area;** ASTA (☞ Travel Agencies, *below*) has a database of specialists worldwide. Do some homework on your own, too: Local tourism boards can provide information about lesser-known and small-niche operators, some of which may sell only direct.

TRAIN TRAVEL

For information on national and regional rail service to New York

City, contact **Amtrak** (☎ 800/872–7245), the **Long Island Railroad** (☎ 718/217–5477), **Metro-North Commuter Railroad** (☎ 212/340–3000), **New Jersey Transit** (☎ 201/762–5100), and **PATH** (☎ 800/234–7284).

TRAVEL AGENCIES

A good travel agent puts your needs first. Look for an agency that has been in business at least five years, emphasizes customer service, and has someone on staff who specializes in your destination. In addition, **make sure the agency belongs to the American Society of Travel Agents** (ASTA). If your travel agency is also acting as your tour operator, *see* Tour Operators, *above*.

➤LOCAL AGENT REFERRALS: **American Society of Travel Agents** (ASTA, ☎ 800/965–2782 24-hr hot line, ℻ 703/684–8319). **Alliance of Canadian Travel Associations** (⊠ 1729 Bank St., Suite 201, Ottawa, Ontario K1V 7Z5, ☎ 613/521–0474, ℻ 613/521–0805). **Association of British Travel Agents** (⊠ 55–57 Newman St., London W1P 4AH, ☎ 0171/637–2444, ℻ 0171/637–0713).

VISITOR INFORMATION

Contact the New York City visitors information offices below for brochures, subway and bus maps, a calendar of events, listings of hotels and weekend hotel packages, and discount coupons for Broadway shows. For a free "I Love New York" booklet listing New York City attractions and tour packages, contact the New York State Division of Tourism.

➤CITY INFORMATION: **New York Convention and Visitors Bureau** (⊠ 2 Columbus Circle, New York, NY 10019, ☎ 212/484–1200, ℻ 212/484–1280), open weekdays 9–5. **New York City Visitors Information Center** (☎ 212/397–8222).

➤STATEWIDE INFORMATION: **New York State Division of Tourism** (⊠ 1 Commerce Ave., Albany, NY 12245, ☎ 518/474–4116 or 800/225–5697).

1 Destination: New York City

DISCOVERING NEW YORK

IN 1925, the youthful song-writing team of Richard Rodgers and Larry Hart wrote "Manhattan," arguably the loveliest city anthem ever. "We'll have Manhattan, the Bronx, and Staten Island, too," it promises, drawing its images from the merry scramble that was the city more than 60 years ago: "sweet push-carts," "baloney on a roll," a subway that "charms," Brighton Beach, Coney Island, and the popular comedy *Abie's Irish Rose*. "We'll turn Manhattan into an isle of joy," coos the refrain.

Several decades later, in 1989, an album called simply *New York,* by aging enfant terrible rocker Lou Reed, viewed the same city with glasses fogged by despair and cynicism: Drugs, crime, racism, and promiscuity reigned in what Reed considered to be a sinkhole of "crudity, cruelty of thought and sound." His voice brittle with weary irony, he sang, "This is no time for celebration." Manhattan's "sweet pushcarts" now apparently overflow with deadly vials of crack.

So, whom to believe—Larry or Lou?

The truth of the matter is slippery, for New York has long been a mosaic of grand contradictions, a city for which there has never been—nor ever will be—a clear consensus. Hart himself took the city to task in another song, "Give It Back to the Indians," whose lyrics count off a litany of problems that still exist: crime, dirt, high prices, traffic jams, and all-around urban chaos. Yet for all that, millions live here, grumbling but happy, and millions more visit, curious as cats to find out what the magnificent fuss is all about.

I was in eighth grade in suburban Detroit when I first really became aware of New York. A friend's Manhattan-born mother subscribed to the Sunday *New York Times,* and at their house I'd pore over the "Arts and Leisure" section, as rapt as an archaeologist with a cave painting. The details of what I read there have blurred, but I remember vividly the sensation I felt while reading: a combined anticipation and nostalgia so keen it bordered on pain. Although I had never been there, I was homesick for New York.

It's my home now, yet I can still appreciate the impulse that draws visitors here. In a city so ripe with possibilities, we are all more or less visitors.

I think of this on an uncharacter-istically warm day in late March, as fellow New Yorkers and I escape from the hives of offices and homes to celebrate spring's first preview. We unbutton our jackets, leave buses a stop or two before our usual destinations, quicken our resolve to visit that new exhibit at the Met or jog around the Central Park Reservoir. A jubilant sense of renewal infects us all, and I overhear one happy fellow saying to a friend, "I felt just like a tourist yesterday."

WHENEVER I get the New York blues, the best tonic for me is to glimpse the city through the eyes of a visitor. One day, after subway construction had rerouted me well out of my usual path, I found myself in the grimy Times Square station—hardly the place for a spiritual conversion. As usual I had that armor of body language that we New Yorkers reflexively assume to protect ourselves from strangers bent on (1) ripping us off, (2) doing us bodily harm, (3) converting us, (4) making sexual advances, or (5) being general pains-in-the-butt just for the hell of it. But that day, tucked away in a corner, was a group of musicians—not an uncommon sight in New York—playing the guitar, organ, and accordion with gusto and good spirits behind a home-made sign that dubbed them the Argentinean Tango Company. Like many other street musicians in Manhattan, they were good, but I was only half listening, too intent on cursing the city. Just as I passed the band, however, I noticed four teenagers drawn to the music—visitors, surely, they were far too open and trusting to be anything else. Grinning as widely as the Argentineans, they began to perform a spontaneous imitation of flamenco dancing—clapping hands above their heads, raising their heels, laughing at themselves, and only slightly self-conscious. Passersby, myself included, broke into smiles. As I made my way to the subway platform, buoyed by the impromptu show, I once again forgave New York. This minor piece of magic was apology enough.

I wonder whether that was the moment one of those teenagers happened to fall in love with the city. It *can* happen in a single moment, to a visitor or to a longtime resident. Perhaps it hits during a stroll through Riverside Park after a blanketing snowfall, when trees have turned to crystal and the city feels a hush it knows at no other time; or when you turn a corner and spy, beyond a phalanx of RVs and a tangle of cables and high-beam lights, the filming of a new movie.

That moment could also come when the house lights dim at the

Metropolitan Opera, and the chandeliers make their magisterial ascent to the ceiling; or when you first glimpse the Prometheus statue in Rockefeller Center, gleaming like a giant present under the annual Christmas tree as dozens of skaters cut swirls of seasonal colors on the ice below. You may even be smitten in that instant when, walking along the streets in the haze of a summer afternoon, you look up above the sea of anonymous faces to see—and be astonished by—the lofty rows of skyscrapers, splendid in their arrogance and power. At times like these it is perfectly permissible to stop for a moment, take a breath, and think, "Wow! *This is New York!*" We who live here do it every so often ourselves.

FOR SOME, of course, that special moment comes when they spot a street or building made familiar by movies or television, from *I Love Lucy* to *On the Waterfront*. At the Empire State Building, who can help but remember King Kong's pathetically courageous swing from its pinnacle? Or at the brooding Dakota, the chilling destiny created for Rosemary's baby within those fortresslike walls? In the mind's eye, Audrey Hepburn is eternally pairing diamonds and a doughnut as she wends her swank way down 5th Avenue to have breakfast at Tiffany's. And the miniature park on Sutton Place will always be where Woody Allen and Diane Keaton began their angst-ridden *Manhattan* love affair, with the 59th Street bridge gleaming beyond and Gershwin music swelling in the background.

There's a moment of sudden magic when a New York stereotype, seen so often on screen that it seems a joke, suddenly comes to life: when a gum-cracking waitress calls you "hon" or a stogie-sucking cabbie asks, "How 'bout them Yankees, Mac?" There's also the thrill of discovering one of New York's cities-within-the-city: Mulberry Street in Little Italy; Mott Street in Chinatown; Park Avenue's enclave of wealth and privilege; SoHo and TriBeCa, with their artistic types dressed in black from head to toe; or Sheridan Square, the nexus of the city's prominent lesbian and gay communities. The first glimpse of a landmark could excite the visitor's infatuation, too: frenetic Grand Central Station, abustle with suburban commuters; the concrete caverns of Wall Street, throbbing with power and ambition; or the Statue of Liberty, which neither cliché nor cheap souvenir can render common.

As you ready yourself to take on New York's contradictions, prepare to wonder and to exult. Here, on a single day, you might catch a glimpse of John Kennedy Jr., or Rollerena, the gloriously tacky drag-queen-cum-fairy-godmother on roller skates, who waves her magic wand to bestow blessings on select public events. Here you can eat sumptuously at a hot-dog stand or at a world-celebrated gourmet shrine.

Excess and deprivation mingle here: As a limousine crawls lazily to take its pampered passengers to their luxe destination, it rolls past a beggar seeking the warmth that steams from the city's belly through an iron grate. It's a ludicrously bright cartoon and a sobering documentary, New York—almost too much for one city to be. It's maddening and it's thrilling; monstrous, yet beautiful beyond parallel.

And I envy anyone their first taste of it.

— Michael Adams

Writer Michael Adams finally moved to his hometown, New York City, 17 years ago.

2 Exploring Manhattan

M

ANHATTAN IS, ABOVE ALL, a
walker's city. Along its busy streets
there's something else to look at
every few yards. Attractions, many of them world-famous,
are crowded close together on this narrow island, and because it has to grow up, not out, new layers are simply piled
on top of the old. The city's character changes every few
blocks, with quaint town houses shouldering sleek glass towers, gleaming gourmet supermarkets sitting around the
corner from dusty thrift shops, and soot-smudged warehouses inhabited at street level by trendy neon-lit bistros.
Many a visitor has been beguiled into walking a little farther, then a little farther still—"Let's just see what that copper dome and steeple belongs to . . ." Now and then, simply
find a bench or ledge to perch on, and take time just to watch
the people passing by. New York has so many faces that
every visitor can discover a different one.

Revised by
Hannah
Borgeson,
David Low,
and
Stephen
Wolf

Orientation

Above 14th Street, the streets form a regular grid pattern
imposed in 1811. Consecutively numbered streets run east
and west (crosstown), while broad avenues, most of them
also numbered, run north (uptown) and south (downtown). The chief exceptions are Broadway (which runs on
a diagonal from East 14th to West 79th Street) and the thor-
oughfares that hug the shores of the Hudson and East
rivers. Many New Yorkers themselves cannot master the
complexities of this system, so in their daily dealings they
usually include cross-street references along with avenue addresses and rely on the Manhattan Address Locator found
in the front of the local phone book.

Below 14th Street—the area that was already settled before the 1811 grid was decreed—Manhattan streets are a
jumble. There's an East Broadway and a West Broadway,
both of which run north–south and neither of which is an
extension of plain old Broadway. Logic won't help you below
14th Street; only a good street map and good directions will.
You may also be confused by the way New Yorkers use "uptown" and "downtown." Unfortunately, there is no con-

sensus about where these areas are: Downtown may mean anyplace from the tip of lower Manhattan through Chelsea; it depends on the orientation of the speaker. A similar situation exists with "East Side" and "West Side." Someone may refer to a location as "on the east side," meaning somewhere east of 5th Avenue. A hotel described as being "on the west side" may be on West 42nd Street. But when New Yorkers speak of the East Side or the West Side, they usually mean the respective areas above 59th Street, on either side of Central Park.

Rockefeller Center and Vicinity

Athens has its Parthenon and Rome its Coliseum. New York's temples, which you see on this mile-long tour along six avenues and five streets, are its concrete-and-glass skyscrapers. Many of them, including the Lever House and the Seagram Building, have been pivotal in the history of modern architecture, and the 19 warm-hued limestone and aluminum buildings of Rockefeller Center are world-renowned.

Sights to See

Numbers in the margin correspond to points of interest on the Midtown map.

❼ American Craft Museum. Distinctions between "craft" and "high art" become irrelevant here, for much of this work created by contemporary American and international artisans is provocative and fun to look at. You may see works in clay, glass, fabric, wood, metal, paper, or even chocolate. ⊠ *40 W. 53rd St.,* ☎ *212/956–3535.* 🎫 *$5.* ☺ *Tues.–Sun. 10–6, Thurs. 10–8.*

Diamond District. The relatively unglitzy jewelry shops at street level on 47th Street between 5th and 6th avenues are just the tip of the iceberg; upstairs, millions of dollars' worth of gems are traded, and skilled craftsmen cut precious stones. Wheeling and dealing goes on at fever pitch, all rendered strangely exotic by the presence of a host of Hasidic Jews in severe black dress, beards, and curled side locks.

❸ GE Building. This 70-story building is the tallest tower in ☞ Rockefeller Center. It was known as the RCA Building until

GE acquired its namesake company in 1986. The block-long street called Rockefeller Plaza, which runs between the GE Building and the Lower Plaza, is officially a private street; each year it is the site of the ever-popular Rockefeller Christmas tree. The thoroughfare is often choked with celebrities' black limousines, for this is the headquarters of the NBC television network. From this building emanated some of the first TV programs ever, including the *Today* show. It's now broadcast from a ground-floor, glass-enclosed studio on the southwest corner of 49th Street and Rockefeller Plaza, so if you're in the area between 7 and 9 AM, your face may show up on TV behind the *Today* show hosts. To see what goes on inside, sign up for a one-hour tour of the NBC Studios. ⊠ *30 Rockefeller Plaza,* ☎ *212/664–7174.* 🎫 *Tour $10. Children under 6 not permitted.* ☉ *Tour departs from street level of GE Bldg. every 15 mins Easter–Labor Day, weekdays 9:30– 6; Sat. 9:30–7; Sun. 9:30–4:45; Thanksgiving–New Year's Day, weekdays 9:30–5; Sat. 9:30–4:30; Sun. 9:30–4:45. Other times of yr, tour departs every ½ hr, weekdays 9:30– 4:30, every 15 mins Sat. 9:30–4:30.*

As you enter the GE Building from Rockefeller Plaza, look up at the striking sculpture of Zeus above the entrance doors, executed in limestone cast in glass by Lee Lawrie, the same artist who sculpted the big Atlas in front of the International Building (☞ Rockefeller Center, *below*) on 5th Avenue. Inside, crane your neck to see the dramatic ceiling mural entitled *Time,* by José Maria Sert. An elevator to the 65th floor will bring you to the **Rainbow Room** (☞ Chapter 3), where you can have drinks or a meal with a spectacular view. ⊠ *Bounded by Rockefeller Plaza, 6th Ave., and 49th and 50th Sts.*

⓼ Lever House. Architect Gordon Bunshaft, of Skidmore, Owings & Merrill, created this seminal skyscraper, a sheer, slim glass box resting on one end of a one-story-thick shelf that is balanced on square chrome columns and seems to float above the street. Because the tower occupies only half of the space above the lower floors, a great deal of airspace is left open, and the tower's side wall displays a reflection of its neighbors. It was built in 1952 to house the offices of the Lever Brothers soap company. ⊠ *390 Park Ave., between 53rd and 54th Sts.*

10

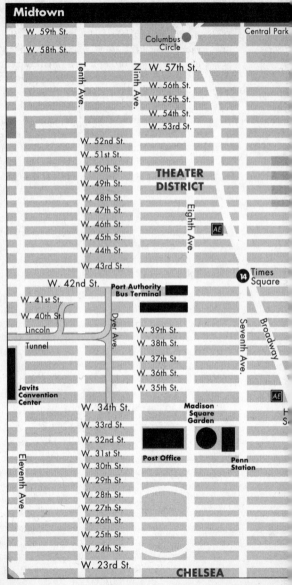

Midtown

Central Park

Columbus Circle

W. 59th St.

W. 58th St.

W. 57th St.

W. 56th St.

W. 55th St.

W. 54th St.

W. 53rd St.

W. 52nd St.

W. 51st St.

W. 50th St.

W. 49th St.

W. 48th St.

W. 47th St.

W. 46th St.

W. 45th St.

W. 44th St.

W. 43rd St.

THEATER DISTRICT

Tenth Ave.

Ninth Ave.

Eighth Ave.

Times Square **14**

W. 42nd St.

Port Authority Bus Terminal

W. 41st St.

W. 40th St.

Lincoln Tunnel

Dyer Ave.

W. 39th St.

W. 38th St.

W. 37th St.

W. 36th St.

W. 35th St.

Seventh Ave.

Broadway

Javits Convention Center

W. 34th St.

W. 33rd St.

W. 32nd St.

W. 31st St.

W. 30th St.

W. 29th St.

W. 28th St.

W. 27th St.

W. 26th St.

W. 25th St.

W. 24th St.

W. 23rd St.

Eleventh Ave.

Madison Square Garden

Post Office

Penn Station

CHELSEA

entral Park S.

E. 59th St.

E. 58th St.

E. 57th St.

E. 56th St.

E. 55th St.

KEY

AE American Express Office

E. 54th St.

E. 53rd St.

E. 52nd St.

E. 51st St.

E. 50th St.

E. 49th St.

E. 48th St.

E. 47th St.

E. 46th St.

E. 45th St.

E. 44th St.

E. 43rd St.

Madison Ave.

Park Ave.

Lexington Ave.

Third Ave.

Vanderbilt Ave.

(Sixth Ave.)

Times Square

E. 42nd St.

Bryant Park (13)

Broadway

Fifth Ave.

Park Ave.

E. 41st St.

E. 40th St.

E. 39th St.

E. 38th St.

Queens-Midtown Tunnel

Tudor City Pl.

E. 37th St.

E. 36th St.

MURRAY HILL

E. 35th St.

Second Ave.

First Ave.

AE

Herald Square

E. 34th St.

E. 33rd St.

E. 32nd St.

E. 31st St.

E. 30th St.

E. 29th St.

E. 28th St.

E. 27th St.

Ave. of the Americas

Lexington Ave.

FDR Dr.

East River

Sutton Pl.

E. 26th St.

E. 25th St.

E. 24th St.

E. 23rd St.

Madison Square

AE

★ ❻ **Museum of Modern Art (MoMA).** In its second- and third-floor galleries of painting and sculpture, MoMA displays some of the world's most famous modern paintings: van Gogh's *Starry Night,* Picasso's *Les Demoiselles d'Avignon,* Matisse's *Dance.* The bright and airy six-story structure, built around a secluded sculpture garden, also houses photography, architecture, decorative arts, drawings, prints, illustrated books, and films. Afternoon and evening film shows, mostly of foreign productions and classics, are free with the price of admission; tickets, distributed in the lobby on the day of the performance, often go fast. Programs change daily; call for a schedule. Free jazz concerts are given in the café on Friday evenings. Leave time to sit outside in that wonderful Sculpture Garden, which hosts contemporary music concerts during the summer. ⊠ *11 W. 53rd St.,* ☎ *212/708–9480; 212/708–9491 for jazz program.* 🖾 *$9.50; pay what you wish Fri. 4:30–8:30.* ☉ *Sat.–Tues. and Thurs. 10:30–6, Fri. 10:30–8:30.*

❺ **Museum of Television and Radio.** Three galleries of photographs and artifacts document the history of broadcasting in this new limestone building by Philip Johnson and John Burgee. But most visitors come here to sit at the museum consoles and watch TV: The collection includes more than 75,000 television shows and radio programs, as well as several thousand commercials. ⊠ *25 W. 52nd St.,* ☎ *212/621–6800 for general information and daily events; 212/621–6600 for other information.* 🖾 *$6 (suggested donation).* ☉ *Tues.–Sun. noon–6, Thurs. noon–8.*

❹ **Radio City Music Hall.** Part of ☞ Rockefeller Center, this 6,000-seat Art Deco masterpiece is America's largest indoor theater, with a 60-ft-high foyer and 2-ton chandeliers. Home of the fabled Rockettes chorus line (which actually started out in St. Louis in 1925), Radio City was built as a movie theater with a stage suitable for live shows as well. Its days as a first-run movie house are long over, but after an announced closing in 1978, Radio City has had an amazing comeback, producing concerts, awards presentations, and special events, along with its own Christmas and Easter extravaganzas. On most days you can take a one-hour tour of the premises. ⊠ *1260 6th Ave., at 50th St.,* ☎ *212/247–4777 or 212/632–4041 for tour information.*

☎ *Tour $13.75.* ⊙ *Tours usually leave from main lobby every 30 mins Mon.–Sat. 10–5, Sun. 11–5.*

★ ❷ **Rockefeller Center.** Begun during the Great Depression of the 1930s by John D. Rockefeller, this 19-building complex occupies nearly 22 acres of prime real estate between 5th and 7th avenues and 47th and 52nd streets. Its central cluster of buildings consist of smooth shafts of warm-hued limestone, streamlined with glistening aluminum. The real genius of the complex's design was its intelligent use of public space: Its plazas, concourses, and street-level shops create a sense of community for the nearly quarter of a million human beings who use it daily. The center itself is a capital of the communications industry, containing the headquarters of a TV network (NBC); major publishing companies (Time-Warner, McGraw-Hill); and the world's largest news-gathering organization, the Associated Press. The complex's major edifices include ☞ **Radio City Music Hall** and the ☞ **GE Building.**

A huge statue of Atlas supporting the world stands sentry before the **International Building** (⊠ 5th Ave. between 50th and 51st Sts.). Just south of the International Building is the **Channel Gardens** (⊠ 5th Ave. between 49th and 50th Sts.), a promenade with six pools surrounded by flower beds filled with seasonal plantings. The Channel Gardens are called so because they separate the British building to the north from the French building to the south (above each building's entrance is a national coat of arms). Looking westward across the Channel Gardens, you will see one of the most famous sights in the complex (if not all of New York): the great gold-leaf statue of the fire-stealing Greek hero Prometheus, sprawled on his ledge above the **Lower Plaza** (⊠ Between 5th and 6th Aves. and 49th and 50th Sts.). A quotation from Aeschylus is carved into the red granite wall behind. The plaza's trademark ice-skating rink is open from October through April; the rest of the year, it becomes an open-air café. ☎ *212/632–3975 for Rockefeller Center information.*

★ ❾ **St. Bartholomew's Church.** Church fathers have been eager to sell the airspace over this 1919 structure with rounded arches and an intricately tiled Byzantine dome, to take advantage of the stratospheric property values in this part of town. So far, fortunately, landmark forces have prevented any such move. ⊠ *Park Ave. between 50th and 51st Sts.*

★ ❶ **St. Patrick's Cathedral.** The Gothic-style house of worship is the Roman Catholic Cathedral of New York. Dedicated to the patron saint of the Irish—then and now one of New York's principal ethnic groups—the white marble and stone structure was begun in 1858, consecrated in 1879, and completed in 1906. The congregation purposely chose the 5th Avenue location for their church, claiming a prestigious spot for themselves at least on Sundays—otherwise they would be in the neighborhood largely as employees of the wealthy. Among the statues in the alcoves around the nave is a modern interpretation of the first American-born saint, Mother Elizabeth Seton. ⊠ *5th Ave. at 50th St.,* ☎ *212/753–2261 rectory.*

42nd Street

As midtown Manhattan's central axis, 42nd Street ties together several major points of interest, passing by Times Square to Grand Central Terminal to the United Nations on the East River. Despite being on one of the world's busiest streets, some of its blocks fell upon hard times over the years. Having acquired a reputation as a den of pickpockets, porno houses, prostitutes, and destitutes, the area is working to reclaim its fame as the metaphorical Broadway. New stores, hotels, and restaurants, many with entertainment themes, are moving in as well. Some critics decry the Disney-fication of this part of town, but really, what area is more appropriate for this over-the-top treatment?

Sights to See

Numbers in the margin correspond to points of interest on the Midtown map.

★ **Bryant Park.** The New York Public Library keeps an incredible stash of books underneath this lovely stretch of green. The park, a haven for the unseemly just several years ago, now teems with well-dressed professionals who fight for lawn chairs for their brown-bag power lunches. Named for the poet and editor William Cullen Bryant

(1794–1878), this was the site of America's first World's Fair, the Crystal Palace Exhibition of 1853–54. The park also has an elegant restaurant and a café.

★ ⓫ **Chrysler Building.** It'd be a shame to make New Yorkers pick one favorite skyscraper, but if they had to, this Art Deco masterpiece (1928–30) would probably be it. The Chrysler Corporation moved out a long time ago, but the building still has its name and many details from the company's cars—check out the elevator cabs, for example. The stainless-steel spire was kept secret during the building's construction so other builders wouldn't know what height to try to top. The building held the world's-tallest title only briefly, as architectural spies found out about it anyway, but it still captivates the eye and the imagination, glistening in the sun during the day, glowing geometrically at night. The Chrysler Building has no observation deck, but you can go into its elegant dark lobby, which is faced with African marble and covered with a ceiling mural that salutes transportation and human endeavor. ⊠ *405 Lexington Ave., at 42nd St.*

★ ⓬ **Grand Central Terminal.** Stop on the south side of 42nd Street to admire the three huge windows separated by columns, and the Beaux Arts clock and sculpture, *Transportation,* crowning the facade above the elevated roadway (Park Avenue is routed around Grand Central's upper story). Go in the side doors on Vanderbilt Avenue to enter the cavernous main concourse, with its 12-story-high ceiling displaying the constellations of the zodiac. Constructed between 1903 and 1913, the building is now being renovated to become a destination in its own right, with more shops and restaurants (à la Union Station in Washington, D.C.). The waiting room by the 42nd Street entrance hosts exhibits and seasonal markets, and musicians often play in the concourse. ⊠ *Main entrance: E. 42nd St. at Park Ave.,* ☎ *212/935–3960. Tours Wed. at 12:30 PM (meet in front of information booth on main level).* ✇ *Tour free (donations to Municipal Art Society accepted).*

★ ⓭ **New York Public Library (NYPL).** This 1911 masterpiece of Beaux Arts design, officially the NYPL's Center for the Humanities, was financed largely by John Jacob Astor. Its grand front steps are guarded by two crouching marble lions—dubbed "Patience" and "Fortitude" by Mayor Fiorello La Guardia, who said he visited the facility to "read between the lions." After admiring the white marble neoclassical facade, walk through the bronze front doors into the grand marble lobby with its sweeping double staircase. Turn left and peek into the DeWitt Wallace Periodicals Room, decorated with trompe l'oeil paintings by Richard Haas to commemorate New York's importance as a publishing center. Then visit changing exhibitions at the art gallery. Among the treasures you might see are Charles Dickens's desk and Thomas Jefferson's own handwritten copy of the Declaration of Independence. Free one-hour tours, each as individual as the library volunteer who leads it, leave from the lobby Monday–Saturday at 11 AM and 2 PM. ✉ *5th Ave. between 40th and 42nd Sts.,* ☎ *212/930–0800.* ☉ *Mon. and Thurs.–Sat. 10–6, Tues.–Wed. 11–7:30 (exhibitions until 6).*

★ ⑭ **Times Square.** Love it or hate it, you can't deny that this is one of New York's principal energy centers. Like many New York City "squares," it's actually triangles formed by the angle of Broadway slashing across a major avenue—in this case, crossing 7th Avenue at 42nd Street. In exchange for having its name grace the area, the *New York Times,* then a less prestigious paper, moved into what had been a relatively quiet area known as Longacre Square when the subway opened. It erected the Times Tower and opened its headquarters here on December 31, 1904 (the building is now resheathed in white marble and called **One Times Square Plaza**), publicizing the event with a fireworks show at midnight and thereby starting a New Year's Eve tradition. Each December 31, a 200-pound ball is lowered down the building's flagpole—a tradition since 1908. From 44th to 51st streets, the cross streets west of Broadway are lined with some 30 major theaters. This has been the city's main theater district since the turn of the century; movie theaters joined the fray beginning in the 1920s. As the theaters drew crowds of people in the evenings, advertisers began to mount huge electric signs here, which gave the intersection its distinctive nighttime glitter.

★ ❿ **United Nations Headquarters.** Now more than 50 years old, this symbol of global cooperation occupies a lushly landscaped 18-acre riverside tract—officially an "international zone" and not part of the United States—just east of 1st Avenue between 42nd and 48th streets. A line of flagpoles with flags arranged in alphabetical order representing the current roster of member nations stands before the striking 550-ft-high slab of the Secretariat Building, with the domed General Assembly Building nestled at its side. The headquarters were designed in 1947–53 by an international team of architects led by Wallace Harrison. You can enter the General Assembly Building at the 46th Street door; the interior corridors overflow with imaginatively diverse artwork donated by member nations. Free tickets to assemblies are sometimes available on a first-come, first-served basis before sessions begin; pick them up in the General Assembly lobby. (The full General Assembly is in session from mid-September to mid-December.) ✉ *Visitor entrance: 1st Ave. and 46th St., ☎ 212/963–7713. ☞ Tour $6.50. ☉ Tours offered daily 9:15–4:45 (weekdays only Jan.–Feb.); 45-min tours in English leave the General Assembly lobby every 20 mins. Children under 5 not permitted.*

Murray Hill and Vicinity

As the city grew progressively north throughout the 19th century, one neighborhood after another had its fashionable heyday, only to fade from glory. But three neighborhoods, east of 5th Avenue roughly between 20th and 40th streets, have preserved much of their historic charm: Murray Hill's brownstone mansions and town houses; Madison Square's classic turn-of-the-century skyscrapers; and Gramercy Park's London-like leafy square.

Sights to See
Numbers in the margin correspond to points of interest on the Midtown Map.

★ ☺ ⓰ **Empire State Building.** It may no longer be the world's tallest building, but it is certainly one of the world's best-loved skyscrapers, its pencil-slim silhouette a symbol for New York City. The Art Deco playground for King Kong opened in 1931 after only about a year and a half of construction. The crowning spire was originally designed as a mooring mast for dirigibles, but none ever docked here; in 1951, a TV transmittal tower was added to the top, raising the total height to 1,472 ft. Today more than 16,000 people work in the building, and more than 2½ million people a year visit the 86th- and 102nd-floor observatories. In 1956 revolving beacons named the Freedom Lights were installed. These lights are illuminated from dusk to midnight. At night, the top 30 stories are illuminated with colors appropriate to the season (green for St. Pat's Day, red and green around Christmas, orange and brown for Halloween). Tickets for the observation decks can be purchased at the concourse level. The 102nd-floor spot is glassed in; the 86th floor is open to the air. ⊠ *350 5th Ave., at 34th St. Observation decks:* ☎ *212/736–3100.* ☒ *$4.50.* ☉ *Daily 9:30 AM–midnight; last elevator up leaves at 11:30 PM. New York Skyride:* ☎ *212/279–9777.* ☒ *$9.* ☉ *Daily 10–10.*

★ ⑰ **Flatiron Building.** Like the Empire State Building and a host of other structures in the city, this was the tallest building in the world when it opened (1902). Architect Daniel Burnham is responsible for the design, which made ingenious use of the triangular plot of land and created very nontraditional office spaces inside—its rounded front point is only 6 ft wide, but gentle waves built into the molded limestone-and-terra-cotta side walls soften the wedge effect. Winds invariably swooped down its 20-story, 286-ft height, billowing up the skirts of women pedestrians on 23rd Street, and local traffic cops had to shoo away male gawkers—coining the phrase "23 Skiddoo." Originally named the Fuller Building, it was instantly rechristened by the public because of its resemblance to a flatiron, and eventually the nickname became official. ⊠ *175 5th Ave., bordered by 22nd and 23rd Sts., 5th Ave., and Broadway.*

★ ⑮ **Pierpont Morgan Library.** The core of this small, patrician museum is the famous banker's own study and library, completed in 1905 by McKim, Mead & White. If you walk east past the museum's main entrance on 36th Street, you'll see the original library's neoclassical facade, with what is believed to be Charles McKim's face on the sphinx in the right-hand sculptured panel. Around the corner, at 37th

Street and Madison Avenue, is the latest addition to the library, an 1852 Italianate brownstone that was once the home of Morgan's son, J. P. Morgan Jr. It's connected to the rest of the property by a glass-roofed garden café court where lunch and afternoon tea are served. The elder Morgan's own house stood at 36th Street and Madison Avenue; it was torn down after his death and replaced with the simple neoclassical annex that today holds the library's main exhibition space. Go inside and visit the galleries for rotating exhibitions; go straight to see items from the permanent collection, principally drawings, prints, manuscripts, and rare books, and to pass through the atrium to the fine bookstore. The most impressive rooms include the elder Morgan's personal study, its red-damask-lined walls hung with first-rate paintings, and his majestic personal library with its dizzying tiers of handsomely bound rare books, letters, and illuminated manuscripts. ⊠ *29 E. 36th St.,* ☎ *212/685–0008.* 🖾 *$5 (suggested donation).* ⊘ *Tues.–Fri. 10:30–5, Sat. 10:30–6, Sun. noon–6.*

Museum Mile

Once known as Millionaire's Row, the stretch of 5th Avenue between 79th and 104th streets has been fittingly renamed Museum Mile, for it now contains an impressive cluster of cultural institutions. The connection is more than coincidental: Many museums are housed in what used to be the great mansions of merchant princes and wealthy industrialists. A large percentage of these buildings were constructed of limestone (it's cheaper than marble) and reflect the Beaux Arts style, which was very popular among the wealthy at the turn of the century.

Sights to See
Numbers in the margin correspond to points of interest on the Museum Mile and Central Park map.

★ ㉙ **Conservatory Garden.** The entrance, at 105th Street, leads through elaborate wrought-iron gates that once graced the mansion of Cornelius Vanderbilt II. The central lawn is bordered by yew hedges and flowering crab-apple trees, leading to a reflecting pool flanked by a large wisteria arbor. To the south is a high-hedged flower garden named after

Frances Hodgson Burnett, author of the children's classic *The Secret Garden*. To the north is the Untermeyer Fountain, with its three spirited girls dancing at the heart of a huge circular bed where 20,000 tulips bloom in the spring and 5,000 chrysanthemums in the fall. ⊠ *Entrance at 105th St. and 5th Ave.* ☉ *Daily 8 AM–dusk.*

㉔ Cooper-Hewitt Museum (officially called the Smithsonian Institution's National Design Museum). Andrew Carnegie sought comfort more than show when he built this 64-room house on what were the outskirts of town in 1901; he administered his extensive philanthropic projects from the first-floor study. (Note the low doorways—Carnegie was only 5 ft 2 inches tall.) The core of the museum's collection was begun in 1897 by the three Hewitt sisters, granddaughters of inventor and industrialist Peter Cooper; major holdings include drawings, prints, textiles, furniture, metalwork, ceramics, glass, woodwork, and wall coverings. ⊠ *2 E. 91st St.,* ☎ *212/860–6868.* 🎟 *$3; free Tues. 5–9.* ☉ *Tues. 10–9, Wed.–Sat. 10–5, Sun. noon–5.*

㉘ El Museo del Barrio. *El barrio* is Spanish for "the neighborhood," and the museum is positioned on the edge of Spanish Harlem, a largely Puerto Rican neighborhood. Though the museum focuses on Latin American and Latino culture, and has objects from the Caribbean and Central and South America, its collection of Puerto Rican art is particularly strong. The 8,000-object permanent collection includes numerous pre-Columbian artifacts. ⊠ *1230 5th Ave., at 104th St.,* ☎ *212/831–7272.* 🎟 *$4 (suggested donation).* ☉ *Wed.–Sun. 11–5; May–Sept., Thurs. until 8.*

★ **⑪ Frick Collection.** Coke-and-steel baron Henry Clay Frick found a home for the superb art collection he was amassing far from the soot and smoke of Pittsburgh, where he'd made his fortune. The mansion was designed by architects Carrère and Hastings (also responsible for the New York Public Library on 5th Avenue at 42nd Street) and built in 1914. Opened as a public museum in 1935 and expanded in 1977, it still resembles a gracious private home, albeit one with a bona fide masterpiece or two in almost every room. Strolling through the mansion, one can imagine how it felt to live with Vermeers by the front stairs, Gainsbor-

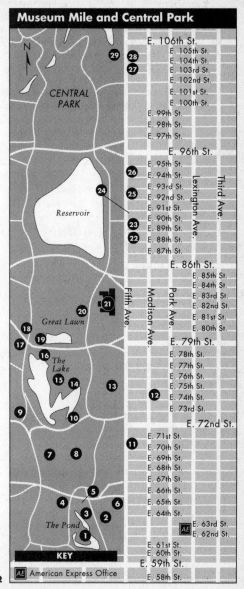

Museum Mile and Central Park

ough and Reynolds portraits in the dining room, canvases by Constable and Turner in the library, and Titians, Holbeins, a Giovanni Bellini, and an El Greco in the living room. ⊠ *1 E. 70th St.,* ☎ *212/288–0700.* ⌧ *$5. Children under 10 not admitted.* ☉ *Tues.–Sat. 10–6, Sun. 1–6.*

㉒ Guggenheim Museum. Frank Lloyd Wright eschewed cities, and this building of his (opened in 1959, shortly after he died) is either praised or criticized. Inside, the assertive six-story spiral rotunda makes for challenging viewing: Under a 92-ft-high glass dome, a ¼-mi-long ramp spirals down past changing exhibitions of modern art. The museum has especially strong holdings in Wassily Kandinsky, Paul Klee, and Pablo Picasso; the oldest pieces are by the French Impressionists. ⊠ *1071 5th Ave., at 88th St.,* ☎ *212/423–3500.* ⌧ *$8, Fri. 6–8 pay as you wish; joint admission to both Guggenheim branches $10.* ☉ *Sun.–Wed. 10–6, Fri.–Sat. 10–8.*

㉖ International Center of Photography (ICP). A relatively young institution—founded in 1974—ICP is building a strong collection of 20th-century photography. Its changing exhibitions often focus on the work of a single prominent photographer or one photographic genre (portraits, architecture, etc.). ⊠ *1130 5th Ave., at 94th St.,* ☎ *212/860–1777.* ⌧ *$4; Tues. 6–8 pay as you wish.* ☉ *Tues. 11–8, Wed.–Sun. 11–6.*

㉕ Jewish Museum. The permanent two-floor exhibition, which complements temporary shows, traces the development of Jewish culture and identity over 4,000 years. The exhibition draws on the museum's enormous collection of artwork, ceremonial objects, and electronic media. The line to get in sometimes extends down the block, so try to arrive early in the day. ⊠ *1109 5th Ave., at 92nd St.,* ☎ *212/423–3230.* ⌧ *$7; Tues. after 5 pay as you wish.* ☉ *Sun.–Mon. and Wed.–Thurs. 11–5:45, Tues. 11–8.*

★ **㉑ Metropolitan Museum of Art.** The quality and range of its holdings make it one of the world's greatest museums. It's the largest art museum in the Western Hemisphere (1.6 million square ft), and its permanent collection of more than 2 million works of art from all over the world includes objects from prehistoric to modern times. The museum, founded in 1870, moved to this location in 1880, but the original redbrick building by Calvert Vaux has since been encased in other architecture. The majestic 5th Avenue facade was built in 1902. The 5th Avenue entrance leads into the Great Hall, a soaring neoclassical chamber that has been designated a landmark. Past the admission booths, a vast marble staircase leads up to the European painting galleries, whose highlights include Botticelli's *The Last Communion of St. Jerome,* Pieter Brueghel's *The Harvesters,* El Greco's *View of Toledo,* Johannes Vermeer's *Young Woman with a Water Jug,* and Rembrandt's *Aristotle with a Bust of Homer.* The arcaded European Sculpture Court includes Auguste Rodin's massive bronze *The Burghers of Calais.* American art has its own wing, back in the northwest corner; the best approach is on the first floor, where you enter through a refreshingly light and airy garden court graced with Tiffany stained-glass windows, cast-iron staircases by Louis Sullivan, and a marble Federal-style facade taken from the Wall Street branch of the United States Bank. Take the elevator to the third floor and begin working your way down through the rooms decorated in period furniture—everything from a Shaker retiring room to a Federal-era ballroom to the living room of a Frank Lloyd Wright house—and the excellent galleries of American painting.

There is much more to the Met than paintings, however. Immediately to the left of the Great Hall on the first floor is Greek and Roman statuary, not to mention a large collection of rare Roman wall paintings excavated from the lava of Mount Vesuvius. Directly above these galleries, on the second floor, you'll find room after room of Grecian urns and other classical vases. The Met's awesome Egyptian collection, spanning some 3,000 years, is on the first floor, directly to the right of the Great Hall. Its centerpiece is the Temple of Dendur, an entire Roman-period temple (circa 15 BC) donated by the Egyptian government in thanks for U.S. help in saving ancient monuments. The Met's medieval collection here is lovely, but to see the real medieval treasures, don't miss a trip to the **Cloisters** (☞ Off the Beaten Path, *below*), the Met's annex in Washington Heights. Although it exhibits only a portion of its vast holdings, the Met offers more than can reasonably be seen in one visit.

Walking tours and lectures are free with your admission contribution. Tours covering various sections of the museum begin about every 15 minutes on weekdays, less frequently on weekends; they depart from the Tour Board in the Great Hall. Self-guided audio tours can also be rented at a desk in the Great Hall. Lectures, often related to temporary exhibitions, are given frequently. ✉ *5th Ave. at 82nd St.,* ☎ *212/879–5500.* ☞ *$8 (suggested donation).* ☉ *Tues.–Thurs. and Sun. 9:30–5:15, Fri.–Sat. 9:30–8:45.*

★ ㉗ **Museum of the City of New York.** From the Dutch settlers of Nieuw Amsterdam to the present day, with period rooms, dioramas, slide shows, films, prints, paintings, sculpture, and clever displays of memorabilia, this museum's got it all. An exhibit on the Port of New York illuminates the role of the harbor in New York's rise to greatness; the noteworthy Toy Gallery has several meticulously detailed dollhouses. ✉ *1220 5th Ave., at 103rd St.,* ☎ *212/534–1672.* ☞ *$5 (suggested donation).* ☉ *Wed.–Sat. 10–5, Sun. 1–5.*

㉓ **National Academy of Design.** The academy, which was founded in 1825, has always required each elected member to donate a representative work of art, which has resulted in a strong collection of 19th- and 20th-century American art. Members have included Mary Cassatt, Samuel F. B. Morse, Winslow Homer, John Singer Sargent, Frank Lloyd Wright, Jacob Lawrence, and Robert Rauschenberg. Changing shows of American art and architecture, some curated by member artists, are drawn from the permanent collection. The collection's home is a stately 19th-century mansion and a pair of town houses. ✉ *1083 5th Ave., at 89th St.,* ☎ *212/369–4880.* ☞ *$5; free Fri. 5–8.* ☉ *Wed.–Sun. noon–5, Fri. until 8.*

⑫ **Whitney Museum of American Art.** This museum grew out of a gallery in the studio of the sculptor and collector Gertrude Vanderbilt Whitney, whose talent and taste were fortuitously accompanied by the wealth of two prominent families. The monolithic exterior is much more forbidding than the interior, where changing exhibitions offer an intelligent survey of 20th-century American works; the second-floor shows, among other exhibits, daring new work from American video artists and filmmakers, and the third-floor gallery features a sample of the permanent collection, including Edward Hopper's haunting *Early Sunday Morning* (1930), Georgia O'Keeffe's *White Calico Flower* (1931), and Jasper Johns's *Three Flags* (1958). ⊠ *945 Madison Ave., at 75th St.,* ☎ *212/570–3676.* ⊡ *$8; free Thurs. 6–8.* ☉ *Wed. and Fri.–Sun. 11–6, Thurs. 1–8.*

Central Park

Without Central Park's 843 acres of meandering paths, tranquil lakes, ponds, and open meadows, New Yorkers might be a lot less sane. Although it appears to be nothing more than a swath of rolling countryside exempted from urban development, Central Park was in fact the first artificially landscaped park in the United States. The design for the park was conceived in 1857 by park superintendent Frederick Law Olmsted and Calvert Vaux, and was one of 33 submitted in a contest arranged by the Central Park Commission—the first such contest in the country. The task of constructing the park was monumental. Hundreds of residents of shantytowns were displaced, swamps were drained, and great walls of Manhattan schist were blasted. Thousands of workers were employed to remove some 5 million cubic yards of soil and plant thousands of trees and shrubs in a project that lasted 16 years and cost $14 million.

Today, Central Park hosts a vast assortment of outdoor activities: jogging, cycling, softball, horseback riding, rock climbing, croquet, tennis, bird watching, boating, chess, checkers, and folk dancing. And if you'd like to experience the park as New Yorkers of the mid-19th century did, you can hire a horse-drawn carriage at Grand Army Plaza or any other major intersection of Central Park South (59th St. between 5th and 8th Aves.). Official rates are $34 for the first half hour and $10 for every additional ¼ hour. Weekends are the liveliest time in the park—free entertainment is on tap, and the entire social microcosm is on parade.

Before you set out for the park, you may want to find out about scheduled events or ranger-led walks and talks. For park information and events, call 212/360–3444. For a schedule of weekend walks and talks led by Urban Park Rangers, call 212/427–4040 or 800/201–7275.

Sights to See

Numbers in the margin correspond to points of interest on the Museum Mile and Central Park map.

⑥ The Arsenal. The park's oldest building, the Arsenal dates from 1857, before Central Park was even created. It occupies a pre–Civil War arsenal and now serves as headquarters of the Parks and Recreation Department. At one time, it was the home of the American Museum of Natural History (☞ The Upper West Side and Morningside Heights, *below*), which is now on Central Park West at 79th Street. The downstairs lobby has some great WPA-era murals; an upstairs gallery features changing exhibitions relating to urban design and natural and organic themes; and a third-floor conference room houses the rendering of the Greensward Plan—the design that Olmsted and Vaux conceived for the park. ☎ 212/360–8111. ☉ *Weekdays 9–4:30.*

⑲ Belvedere Castle. Standing regally atop Vista Rock, Belvedere Castle was built in 1872 of the same gray Manhattan schist that thrusts out of the soil in dramatic outcrops throughout the park. Since 1919 it has been a measurement station of the U.S. Weather Bureau; look up to see the twirling meteorological instruments atop the tower. Climb out onto its balconies for a dramatic view. On the ground floor, the Henry Luce Nature Observatory has nature exhibits, children's workshops, and educational programs. ☎ 212/772–0210. ☜ *Free.* ☉ *Mid-Feb.–mid-Oct., Tues.–Sun. 11–5; mid-Oct.–mid-Feb., Tues.–Sun. 11–4.*

★ ⑩ Bethesda Fountain. Built in 1863 to commemorate the soldiers who died at sea during the Civil War, the ornate, three-tiered Bethesda Fountain was named after the biblical Bethesda pool in Jerusalem, which was supposedly given healing powers by an angel—hence the statue of an angel rising from the center. This statue, called *The Angel of the Waters,* figured prominently in Tony Kushner's epic drama *Angels in America.*

⑯ Bow Bridge. This splendid cast-iron bridge arches over a neck of the Lake to the ☞ **Ramble.** Stand here to take in the picture-postcard view of the water reflecting a quintessentially New York image of vintage apartment buildings peeping above the treetops.

★ ☚ ❹ **Carousel.** Remarkable for the size of its hand-carved steeds—all 57 of them are three-quarters the size of real horses—this carousel was built in 1903 and later moved here from Coney Island. Today it's considered one of the best examples of turn-of-the-century folk art. ☎ *212/879–0244.* 🎟 *90¢. ☉ Summer, weekdays 10:30–8, weekends 10:30–6:30; winter, weekends 10–4, weather permitting.*

☚ ❷ **Central Park Zoo.** Recently renamed the Central Park Wildlife Center, the zoo is a small but delightful menagerie. Clustered around the central Sea Lion Pool are separate exhibits for each of the earth's major environments; the Polar Circle features a huge penguin tank and polar-bear floe; the open-air Temperate Territory has a pit of chattering monkeys; and the Tropic Zone contains the flora and fauna of a miniature rain forest. ✉ *Entrance at 5th Ave. and 64th St.,* ☎ *212/439–6500.* 🎟 *$2.50. No children under 16 admitted without adult. ☉ Apr.–Oct., weekdays 10–5, weekends 10:30–5:30; Nov.–Mar., daily 10–4:30.*

❷⓪ **Cleopatra's Needle.** This exotic, hieroglyphic-covered obelisk was a gift to the city in 1881 from the khedive of Egypt.

☚ ⓭ **Conservatory Water.** At the symmetrical stone basin of this neo-Renaissance-style concrete basin you can watch some very sophisticated model boats being raced each Saturday morning at 10. (Model boats are occasionally for rent here.) At the north end is one of the park's most beloved statues, José de Creeft's 1960 bronze sculpture of **Alice in Wonderland.** On the west side of the pond, a bronze statue of **Hans Christian Andersen** is the site of storytelling hours on summer weekends.

❺ **The Dairy.** As its name implies, this was originally an actual dairy built in the 19th century, when cows grazed in the area. Today the Dairy's painted, pointed eaves, steeple, and high-pitched slate roof harbor the park's visitor center. Here you can buy maps and souvenirs, and a small research library lends out books about the park. ☎ *212/794–6565. ☉ Winter, Tues.–Sun. 11–4; summer, Tues.–Sun. 11–5.*

🕒 **Delacorte Clock.** Set above a redbrick arch near the Central Park Zoo, this delightful glockenspiel was dedicated to the city by philanthropist George T. Delacorte. Its fanciful bronze face is decorated with a menagerie of mechanical animals, including a dancing bear, a kangaroo, a penguin, and monkeys that rotate and hammer their bells when the clock chimes its tune every half hour.

Great Lawn. This newly sodded 15-acre expanse of green was scheduled to reopen in 1997 after a two-year, $18 million restoration. The area hums with action on weekends and most summer evenings, when its softball fields and picnicking grounds provide a much-needed outlet for city dwellers of all ages.

⑭ **Loeb Boathouse.** At the brick neo-Victorian boathouse you can rent bicycles as well as boats. Loeb also has a better-than-average restaurant, the Boathouse Cafe. 🚣 *Boat rental $10 per hr, $30 deposit;* ☎ *212/517–4723.* 🚲 *Bicycle rental $8– $10 per hr, tandems $14 per hr, deposit required;* ☎ *212/861– 4137.* ☉ *Mar.–Nov., weekdays 10–6, weekends 9–6, weather permitting. Boathouse Cafe:* ☎ *212/517–2233.* ☉ *Mar.- Sept., Tues.–Fri. noon–4, weekends 11:30–dusk.*

⑧ **The Mall.** A broad, formal walkway where fashionable ladies and men used to gather to see and be seen around the turn of the century, the Mall looks as grand as ever. The southern end of its main path, the **"Literary Walk,"** is covered by the canopy of the largest group of American elms in the Northeast and lined by statues of famous men of letters, including Shakespeare, Robert Burns, and Sir Walter Scott.

Naturalists' Walk. Starting at the new 79th Street entrance to the park across from the Museum of Natural History, this recently created nature walk has a stream that attracts countless species of birds, a woodland area with various native trees, stepping-stone trails that lead over rocky bluffs, and a sitting area.

❶ **The Pond.** Swans and ducks can sometimes be spotted on the calm waters of the Pond. For an unbeatable view of the city skyline, walk along the shore to **Gapstow Bridge.**

⑮ **The Ramble.** Across the Bow Bridge from the Lake, the Ramble is a heavily wooded, wild 37-acre area laced with twisting, climbing paths, designed to resemble upstate New York's Adirondack Mountain region. This is prime bird-watching territory; it shelters many of the more than 260 species of birds that have been sighted in the park. Because it is so dense and isolated, however, it is not a good place to wander alone.

⑱ **Shakespeare Garden.** One of the park's few formal flower plantings, this lushly landscaped, terraced hill is one of the more hidden spots in the park.

➐ **Sheep Meadow.** Used as a sheep grazing area until 1934, this grassy 15-acre meadow is now a favorite of picnickers, sunbathers, and people seeking relaxation. It's an officially designated quiet zone; the most vigorous sports allowed are kite-flying and Frisbee-tossing. The Moorish-style **Mineral Springs Pavillion** at the northern end of Sheep Meadow was built as one of the park's four refreshment stands in the late 1860s. Behind the pavillion are the **Croquet Grounds** and **Lawn Bowling Greens.** During the season (May–November) you can peer through gaps in the hedges to watch the players, usually dressed in crisp white. Just west of the meadow, the famous **Tavern on the Green,** originally the sheepfold, was erected by Boss Tweed in 1870 and is now considered one of the glitziest, kitschiest restaurants in Manhattan.

★ ➒ **Strawberry Fields.** Called the "international peace garden," this memorial to John Lennon is one of the most visited sights in the park. Climbing up a hill, its curving paths, shrubs, trees, and flower beds—all donated from nearly every country of the world—create a deliberately informal pastoral landscape. Just beyond the trees, at 72nd Street and Central Park West, is the Dakota (☞ The Upper West Side and Morningside Heights, *below*), where Lennon lived at the time of his death in 1980.

☝ ⑰ **Swedish Cottage.** Looking like something straight out of Germany's Black Forest, this dark-wood chalet is used for marionette shows. ☎ *212/988–9093.* ☞ *$5.* ☉ *Shows Tues.–Fri. 10:30 and noon; Sat. noon and 3; call for reservations.*

🐾 ❸ **Wollman Memorial Rink.** Even if you don't want to join in, you can stand on the terrace here to watch ice-skaters throughout the winter and roller skaters in the summer. ☎ *212/396–1010.* 💺 *$7, skate rentals and lockers extra.* ☉ *Mid-Oct.–Mar., Mon. 10–4, Tues.–Thurs. 10–9:30, Fri. 10 AM–11 PM, weekends 10–9 for ice-skating; late Apr.–Sept., hrs are approximately the same for in-line skating. Call to confirm prices and hrs, as dates are subject to change due to weather.*

The Upper West Side and Morningside Heights

The Upper West Side has never been as fashionable as the East Side. It has always had an earthier appeal, even though it, too, has had many famous residents, past and present, along with a similar mix of real estate—large apartment buildings along Central Park West, West End Avenue, and Riverside Drive, and town houses on the shady, quiet cross streets—much of which is now protected by landmark status. Once a haven for the Jewish intelligentsia, and still a liberal stronghold, the West Side in the 1960s had become a rather grungy multiethnic community. A slow process of gentrification began in the 1970s, when actors, writers, and gays began to move into the area. Today this neighborhood is quite desirable, with lots of restored brownstones and high-priced co-op apartments.

In Morningside Heights, just north and west of Central Park, a cultural outpost grew up at the end of the 19th century, spearheaded by a triad of institutions: the relocated Columbia University, which developed the mind; St. Luke's Hospital, which cared for the body; and the Cathedral of St. John the Divine, which tended the soul. Idealistically conceived of as an American Acropolis, the cluster of academic and religious institutions that developed here managed to keep these blocks stable during years when neighborhoods on all sides were collapsing. A student neighborhood, the area has a casual atmosphere that is hip, friendly, and fun.

Sights to See

Numbers in the margin correspond to points of interest on the Upper West Side map.

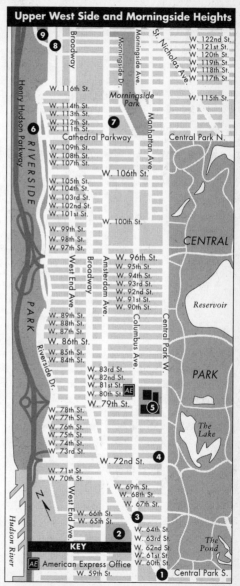

Upper West Side and Morningside Heights

W. 122nd St.
W. 121st St.
W. 120th St.
W. 119th St.
W. 118th St.
W. 117th St.

W. 116th St.

W. 115th St.

Broadway

St. Nicholas Ave.

Morningside Dr.

Morningside Ave.

Morningside Park

Manhattan Ave.

W. 114th St.
W. 113th St.
W. 112th St.
W. 111th St.

Cathedral Parkway

Central Park N.

W. 109th St.
W. 108th St.
W. 107th St.

W. 106th St.

Henry Hudson Parkway

R I V E R S I D E

P A R K

Riverside Dr.

W. 105th St.
W. 104th St.
W. 103rd St.
W. 102nd St.
W. 101st St.

W. 100th St.

W. 99th St.
W. 98th St.
W. 97th St.

West End Ave.

Broadway

Amsterdam Ave.

Columbus Ave.

Central Park W.

W. 96th St.
W. 95th St.
W. 94th St.
W. 93rd St.
W. 92nd St.
W. 91st St.
W. 90th St.

W. 89th St.
W. 88th St.
W. 87th St.

W. 86th St.

W. 85th St.
W. 84th St.

W. 83rd St.
W. 82nd St.
W. 81st St.
W. 80th St.
W. 79th St.

W. 78th St.
W. 77th St.
W. 76th St.
W. 75th St.
W. 74th St.
W. 73rd St.

W. 72nd St.

W. 71st St.
W. 70th St.

W. 69th St.
W. 68th St.
W. 67th St.

West End Ave.

W. 66th St.
W. 65th St.

W. 64th St.
W. 63rd St.
W. 62nd St.
W. 61st St.
W. 60th St.

W. 59th St.

CENTRAL

Reservoir

PARK

The Lake

The Pond

Central Park S.

Hudson River

N

KEY

AE American Express Office

★ ⟨ ❺ **American Museum of Natural History.** With a collection of more than 30 million artifacts, the museum displays something for every taste, from a 94-ft blue whale to the 563-carat Star of India sapphire. Among the most enduringly popular exhibits are the wondrously detailed dioramas of animal habitat groups, on the first and second floors, and the fourth-floor halls full of dinosaur skeletons. Even if you don't want to visit the museum, you should look into **Theodore Roosevelt Rotunda**, a massive marble-laden, barrel-vaulted space where a five-story-tall cast of Barosaurus rears on its hind legs, protecting its fossilized baby from a fossil allosaurus. The **Hayden Planetarium** is closed for replacement by a new building, which will not be completed until 1999. ⊠ *Central Park W, at 79th St.,* ☎ *212/769–5200 for museum tickets and programs, 212/769–5100 for museum general information, 212/769–5034 for IMAX Theater show times.* 🎟 *Museum $8 (suggested donation), IMAX Theater $12; combination tickets available.* ☉ *Sun.–Thurs. 10–5:45; Fri.–Sat. 10–8:45.*

★ ❼ **Cathedral of St. John the Divine.** When New York's major Episcopal church is completed, it will be the world's largest Gothic cathedral; until then, you can have a rare, fascinating look at a cathedral in progress. Work on this immense limestone-and-granite church has progressed in spurts. Its first cornerstone was laid in 1892 and its second in 1925, but with the United States' entry into World War II, construction came to a "temporary" halt that lasted until 1982. St. John's follows traditional Gothic engineering—it is supported by stonemasonry rather than by a steel skeleton—so new stonecutters, many of them youngsters from nearby Harlem neighborhoods, had to be trained before work could proceed. A model in the **gift shop** shows what the cathedral might look like when completed, probably quite a few years into the future.

The vast nave, the length of two football fields (601 ft, actually), can hold 6,000 worshipers. The altar area expresses the cathedral's interfaith tradition and international mission—with menorahs, Shinto vases, golden chests presented by the king of Siam, and in the ring of chapels behind the altar, dedications to various ethnic groups. The **Saint Saviour Chapel** contains a three-panel plaster altar with religious scenes by New York artist Keith Haring. (This was his last work; he died of AIDS in 1990.) Along with Sunday services (8, 9, 9:30, 11 AM, and 1 and 7 PM), the cathedral operates community outreach programs, has changing museum and art gallery displays, supports artists-in-residence and an early-music consortium, and presents a full calendar of nonreligious concerts. Regular tours are offered, including a vertical tour, which climbs 124 ft up a spiral staircase to the top. ⊠ *1047 Amsterdam Ave., at 112th St.,* ☎ *212/316–7540 or 212/662–2133 for box office; 212/932–7347 to arrange tours.* ⊙ *Mon.–Sat. 7–6, Sun. 7 AM–8 PM; tours Tues.–Sat. at 11, Sun. at 1; vertical tours 1st and 3rd Sat. of month at noon and 2.* ⊠ *Tours $3 (suggested donation), vertical tours $10 (suggested donation).*

ℭ The **Children's Museum of Manhattan** is a kind of indoor playground for kids 1–10, where they can climb, crawl, paint, make collages, try on costumes, and even film their own newscasts. Daily workshops are included in the admission price. ⊠ *212 W. 83rd St.,* ☎ *212/721–1234.* ⊠ *$5 adults and children.* ⊙ *Mon. and Wed.–Thurs. 1:30–5:30, Fri.–Sun. 10–5.*

❶ Columbus Circle. This confusing intersection has never had the grandeur or the definition of Broadway's major intersections to the south, but it does have a 700-ton monument capped by a statue of Christopher himself in the middle of a traffic island; it had to be elaborately supported when the land underneath was torn up during the construction of the Columbus Circle subway station in the early 1900s.

★ **❹ The Dakota.** People once thought this building was so far from the city that it might as well have been in the Dakotas; that's how the structure got its name. Indeed, the picturesque gables here housed some of the West Side's first residents, and their remarkable home (built 1880–84) set a high standard for the apartment building that followed. A sort of buff-color château, with copper turrets, the Dakota is often depicted in scenes of Old New York, and it was by looking out of a window here that Si Morley was able to travel back in time in Jack Finney's *Time and Again.* Its slightly spooky appearance was played up in the movie *Rosemary's Baby,* which was filmed here. At the gate on

72nd Street, in December 1980, a deranged fan shot John Lennon as he came home from a recording session. Other celebrity tenants have included Boris Karloff, Rudolf Nureyev, José Ferrer and Rosemary Clooney, Lauren Bacall, Rex Reed, and Gilda Radner. ⊠ *1 W. 72nd St., at Central Park W.*

❾ Grant's Tomb. Civil War general and two-term president Ulysses S. Grant and his wife, Julia Dent Grant, are buried here. The white mausoleum, constructed of more than 8,000 tons of granite, with imposing columns and a classical pediment, is modeled on a number of other famous mausoleums. It opened in 1897, almost 12 years after Grant's death—his remains sat in a temporary brick vault until the monument was completed. ⊠ *Riverside Dr. and 122nd St.,* ☏ *212/666–1640.* ▱ *Free.* ☉ *Daily 9–5, 15- to 20-min tours free on request.*

★ **❷ Lincoln Center.** A neighborhood was razed when Lincoln Center was built during the 1960s (*West Side Story* was filmed on the slum's gritty, deserted streets just before the demolition crews moved in), but that has long been forgotten by the artists who've since moved to the area, as well as their patrons.

Stand on Broadway, facing the central court with its huge fountain. The three concert halls on this plaza, designed by three different architects, clearly relate to one another, with their rhythmical bilevel facades, yet each has different lines and details. On the left, huge honeycomb lights hang on the portico of Philip Johnson's **New York State Theater,** home to the New York City Ballet and the New York City Opera. Straight ahead, at the rear of the plaza, is Wallace Harrison's **Metropolitan Opera House,** its brilliant-colored Chagall murals visible through the arched lobby windows; the Metropolitan Opera and American Ballet Theatre perform here. To your right, abstract bronze sculptures distinguish Max Abramovitz's **Avery Fisher Hall,** host to the New York Philharmonic Orchestra. Wander through the plaza, and then angle to your left between the New York State Theater and the Metropolitan Opera House into **Damrosch Park,** where summer open-air festivals are often accompanied by free concerts at the **Guggenheim Bandshell.**

An overpass leads from this plaza across 65th Street to the world-renowned **Juilliard School** for music and theater. Visitors can wander freely through the lobbies of all these buildings. One-hour guided "Introduction to Lincoln Center" tours, given daily, cover the center's history and wealth of artwork and usually visit the three principal theaters, performance schedules permitting. ☎ 212/875–5000 *for general information, 212/875–5350 for tour schedule and reservations.* 🎫 *Tour $8.25.*

❸ Museum of American Folk Art. Changing exhibits here can be fascinating, and the museum is small enough to absorb in a short period of time. Its collection includes arts and crafts from all over the Americas: native paintings, quilts, carvings, dolls, trade signs, painted wood carousel horses, and a giant Indian-chief copper weather vane. ✉ *2 Lincoln Sq. (Columbus Ave. between 65th and 66th Sts.),* ☎ *212/595–9533.* 🎫 *$3 (suggested donation).* ⊙ *Tues.–Sun. 11:30–7:30.*

New York Convention and Visitors Bureau. This weird pseudo-Byzantine structure was ostensibly modeled after the Doge's Palace in Venice but is locally nicknamed the Lollipop Building. Count on the bureau for brochures; bus and subway maps; hotel, restaurant, and shopping guides; a seasonal calendar of events; free TV-show tickets (sometimes) and discounts on Broadway theater; and sound advice. ✉ *2 Columbus Circle,* ☎ *212/397–8200.* ⊙ *Weekdays 9–6, weekends 10–3.*

★ ❽ Riverside Church. In this modern (1930) Gothic-style edifice, the smooth, pale limestone walls seem the antithesis of the rough gray hulk of the Cathedral of St. John the Divine (☞ *above*). If you're here on Sunday, take the elevator to the top of the 22-story, 356-ft **tower,** with its 74-bell carillon, the largest in the world. ✉ *Riverside Dr. and 122nd St.,* ☎ *212/870–6700.* ⊙ *Mon.–Sat. 9–5, Sun. noon–4; service Sun. 10:45; tower Tues.–Sat. 11–4, Sun. noon–6.* 🎫 *Church free, tower $1.*

❻ Riverside Park. Long and narrow, Riverside Park runs along the Hudson all the way from 72nd Street to 159th Street. The **Promenade,** a broad formal walkway with a stone parapet looking out over the river, extends from 80th Street to a few blocks north. Descend the steps here and go through the underpass beneath Riverside Drive to reach the **79th Street Boat Basin**, a rare spot in Manhattan where you can walk right along the river's edge, smell the salt air, and watch a flotilla of houseboats bobbing in the water.

Greenwich Village

Greenwich Village, which New Yorkers almost invariably speak of simply as "the Village," enjoyed a raffish reputation for years. Originally a rural outpost of the city—a haven for New Yorkers during early 19th-century smallpox and yellow fever epidemics—many of its blocks still look somewhat pastoral, with brick town houses and low rises, tiny green parks and hidden courtyards, and a crazy-quilt pattern of narrow, tree-lined streets. In the mid-19th century, however, as the city spread north of 14th Street, the Village became the province of immigrants, bohemians, and students (New York University, today the nation's largest private university, was planted next to Washington Square in 1831). Its politics were radical and its attitudes tolerant, which is one reason it remains a home to such a large gay community. Today Village apartments and town houses go for high rents, and several posh restaurants have put down roots there. Except for the isolated western fringe, where a string of tough gay bars along West Street attract some drug traffic and prostitution, the Village is about as safe and clean as the Upper East Side. The Village is no longer dangerous, but it still feels bohemian.

Several generations of writers and artists have lived and worked here: in the 19th century, Henry James, Edgar Allan Poe, Mark Twain, Walt Whitman, and Stephen Crane; at the turn of the century, O. Henry, Edith Wharton, Theodore Dreiser, and Hart Crane; and during the 1920s and '30s, John Dos Passos, Norman Rockwell, Sinclair Lewis, John Reed, Eugene O'Neill, Edward Hopper, and Edna St. Vincent Millay. In the late 1940s and early 1950s, the Abstract Expressionist painters Franz Kline, Jackson Pollock, Mark Rothko, and Willem de Kooning congregated here, as did the Beat writers Jack Kerouac, Allen Ginsberg, and Lawrence Ferlinghetti. The 1960s brought folk musicians and poets, notably Bob Dylan and Peter, Paul, and Mary.

Sights to See

Numbers in the margin correspond to points of interest on the Greenwich Village map.

Christopher Park. Sometimes mistaken for Sheridan Square, this pleasant triangular oasis contains a bronze statue of Civil War general Philip Sheridan and striking sculptures designed by George Segal of a lesbian couple sitting on a bench and gay male partners standing near them. ⊠ *Bordered by Washington Pl. and Grove and Christopher Sts.*

❼ 51 Christopher Street. On June 27, 1969, a gay bar at this address named the Stonewall Inn was the site of a clash between gay men (some in drag) and the New York City police. As these men were being forced into paddy wagons, sympathetic gay onlookers protested and started fighting back, throwing beer bottles and garbage cans. The Stonewall Riot is now commemorated each year in several American cities at the end of June with parades and celebrations that honor the gay rights movement. A clothing store now occupies the site of the event; a more recent bar named Stonewall is next door at No. 53.

★ ☙ ❸ Forbes Magazine Galleries. The late publisher Malcolm Forbes's idiosyncratic personal collection fills the ground floor of the limestone Forbes Magazine Building, once the home of Macmillan Publishing. Exhibits change in the large painting gallery and one of two autograph galleries, while permanent highlights include U.S. presidential papers, more than 500 intricate model boats, 12,000 toy soldiers, and some of the oldest Monopoly game sets ever made. Perhaps the most memorable permanent display contains exquisite items created by the House of Fabergé, including 12 jeweled eggs designed for the last of the Russian czars. ⊠ *62 5th Ave., at 12th St., ☎ 212/206–5548. ☞ Free. ☺ Tues.–Wed. and Fri.–Sat. 10–4.*

Gay Street. A curved lane lined with small row houses circa 1810, one-block-long Gay Street was originally a black neighborhood and later a strip of speakeasies. Ruth McKinney created her somewhat zany tales about life in Greenwich Village in the basement of No. 14, and they appeared in book form as *My Sister Eileen* in 1938. Also on

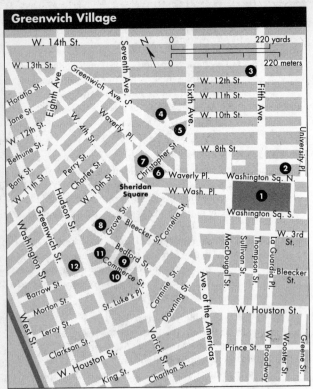

Greenwich Village

Gay Street, Howdy Doody was designed in the basement of No. 12. ⊠ *Between Christopher St. and Waverly Pl.*

⓫ Grove Court. This enclave of brick-front town houses was built between 1853 and 1854. Intended originally as apartments for employees at neighborhood hotels, Grove Court used to be called Mixed Ale Alley because of the residents' propensity to pool beverages brought from work. It now houses a more affluent crowd. ⊠ *10–12 Grove St.*

❾ Isaacs-Hendricks House. Originally built as a Federal-style wood-frame residence in 1799, this immaculate structure is the oldest remaining house in Greenwich Village. Its first owner, Joshua Issacs, a wholesale merchant, lost the farmhouse to creditors; the building then belonged to copper supplier Harmon Hendricks. The village landmark was remodeled twice; it received its brick face in 1836, and the third floor was added in 1928. ⊠ *77 Bedford St., at Commerce St.*

❺ Jefferson Market Library. Critics variously termed this magnificent towered courthouse's hodgepodge of styles Venetian, Victorian, or Italian; Villagers, noting the alternating wide bands of red brick and narrow strips of granite, dubbed it the Lean Bacon Style. Over the years, the structure has housed a number of government agencies (public works, civil defense, census bureau, police academy); it was on the verge of demolition when public-spirited citizens saved it and turned it into a public library in 1967. Note the fountain at the corner of West 10th Street and 6th Avenue, and the seal of the City of New York on the east front; inside, look at the handsome interior doorways and climb the graceful circular stairway. If the gate is open, visit the flower garden behind the library, a project run by local green thumbs. ⊠ *425 6th Ave., at 10th St.,* ☎ *212/243-4334.*

❻ Northern Dispensary. Constructed for $4,700 in 1831, this triangular Georgian brick building originally served as a health-care clinic for indigent Villagers. Edgar Allan Poe was a frequent patient. In more recent times, the structure has housed a dental clinic and a nursing home for AIDS patients. ⊠ *165 Waverly Pl.*

❹ Patchin Place. This charming cul-de-sac off 10th Street (between Greenwich and 6th Aves.) has 10 miniature row houses dating from 1848. Around the corner on 6th Avenue is a similar dead-end street, **Milligan Place**, consisting of four small homes completed in 1852. The houses in both quiet enclaves were originally built for the waiters (mostly Basques) who worked at the high-society Brevoort Hotel, long ago demolished, on 5th Avenue. Patchin Place later became home to several writers, including Theodore Dreiser, e. e. cummings, Jane Bowles, and Djuna Barnes. Milligan Place eventually became the address for several playwrights, including Eugene O'Neill.

★ **❷ The Row.** Built from 1829 through 1839, this series of beautifully preserved Greek Revival town houses along Washington Square North (on the two blocks between University Pl. and MacDougal St.) once belonged to merchants and bankers; now the buildings serve as New York University offices and faculty housing. Developers were not so tactful when they demolished 18 Washington Square North, once the home of Henry James's grandmother, which he later used as the setting for his novel *Washington Square* (Henry himself was born just off the square, in a long-gone house on Washington Place). The oldest building on the block, 20 Washington Square North, was constructed in 1829 in the Federal style. Notice its Flemish bond brickwork—alternate bricks inserted with the smaller surface (headers) facing out—which before 1830 was considered the best way to build stable walls. ✉ *1–13 Washington Sq. N, between University Pl. and 5th Ave.; 19–26 Washington Sq. N, between 5th Ave. and MacDougal St.*

★ **⑫ St. Luke's-in-the-Fields.** The first warden of St. Luke's, which was constructed in 1822 as a country chapel for downtown's Trinity Church, was Clement (" 'Twas the Night Before Christmas") Clarke Moore. An unadorned structure of soft-colored brick, the chapel was nearly destroyed by fire in 1981, but a flood of donations, many quite small, from residents of the West Village financed restoration of the square central tower. ✉ *485 Hudson St., between Barrow and Christopher Sts.*

★ **St. Luke's Place.** This often peaceful street has 15 classic Italianate brownstone and brick town houses (1852–53), shaded by graceful gingko trees. Novelist Theodore Dreiser wrote *An American Tragedy* at No. 16, and poet Marianne Moore resided at No. 14. Mayor Jimmy Walker (first elected in 1926) lived at No. 6; the lampposts in front are "mayor's lamps," which were sometimes placed in front of the residences of New York mayors. This block is often used as a film location, too: No. 12 was shown as the Huxtables' home on *The Cosby Show* (although the family supposedly lived in Brooklyn), and No. 4 was the setting of the Audrey Hepburn movie *Wait Until Dark*. Before 1890 the playground on the south side of the street was a graveyard where, according to legend, the dauphin of France—the lost son of Louis XVI and Marie Antoinette—is buried. ⊠ *Between Hudson St. and 7th Ave. S.*

❿ **75½ Bedford Street.** Rising real-estate rates inspired the construction of New York City's narrowest house—just 9½ ft wide—in 1873. It was built on a lot that was originally a carriage entrance of the Isaacs-Hendricks House next door. Several celebrities have resided in this sliver of a building, including actor John Barrymore and poet Edna St. Vincent Millay, who wrote the Pulitzer Prize–winning *Ballad of the Harp-Weaver* during her stay here from 1923 to 1924. ⊠ *75½ Bedford St., between Commerce and Morton Sts.*

❽ **Twin Peaks.** In 1925 financier Otto Kahn gave money to a Village eccentric named Clifford Daily to remodel an 1835 house for artists' use. The building was whimsically altered with stucco, half-timbers, and the addition of a pair of steep roof peaks. The result was something that might be described as an ersatz Swiss chalet. ⊠ *102 Bedford St., between Grove and Christopher Sts.*

★ **Washington Arch.** Designed by Stanford White, a wood version of Washington Arch was built in 1889 to commemorate the 100th anniversary of George Washington's presidential inauguration and was originally placed about half a block north of its present location. The arch was reproduced in marble in 1892, and the statues—*Washington at War* on the left, *Washington at Peace* on the right—were added in 1916 and 1918, respectively. Bodybuilder Charles

Atlas modeled for *Peace.* ⊠ *Washington Sq., at south end of 5th Ave.*

★ ❶ **Washington Square.** The highly popular 9½-acre park started out as a cemetery, principally for yellow-fever victims, and an estimated 10,000–22,000 bodies lie below. In the early 1800s it was a parade ground and the site of public executions; bodies dangled from a conspicuous Hanging Elm that still stands at the northwest corner of the square. Later Washington Square became the focus of a fashionable residential neighborhood and a center of outdoor activity. By the early 1980s, Washington Square had deteriorated but community activism motivated a police crackdown that made Washington Square somewhat more comfortable again for Frisbee players, street musicians, skateboarders, jugglers, stand-up comics, sitters, strollers, and chess players. ⊠ *At south end of 5th Ave.*

SoHo

Today the name SoHo is virtually synonymous with a certain eclectic elegance—an amalgam of black-clad artists, young Wall Streeters, track-lit loft apartments, hip art galleries, and restaurants with a minimalist approach to both food and decor. It's all very urban, very cool, very now. Twenty-five years ago, this area was a virtual wasteland. SoHo (so named because it is the district *So*uth of *Ho*uston Street, bounded by Broadway, Canal Street, and 6th Avenue) was regularly referred to as "Hell's Hundred Acres" because of the many fires that raged through the untended warehouses crowding the area. It was saved by two factors: (1) preservationists here discovered the world's greatest concentration of cast-iron architecture and fought to prevent demolition; and (2) artists discovered the large, cheap, well-lit spaces that cast-iron buildings provide.

All the rage between 1860 and 1890, cast-iron buildings were popular because they did not require massive walls to bear the weight of the upper stories. Consequentially, these buildings had more interior space and larger windows. They were also versatile, with various architectural elements produced from standardized molds to mimic any style—Italianate, Victorian Gothic, neo-Grecian, to name but a few visible in SoHo. At first it was technically illegal for artists to live in their loft studios, but so many did that eventually the zoning laws were changed to permit residence. By 1980 SoHo's galleries, trendy shops, and cafés, together with its marvelous cast-iron buildings and vintage Belgianblock pavements (the 19th-century successor to traditional cobblestones), had made SoHo such a desirable residential area that only the most successful artists could afford it. Today, the arrival of large chain stores such as Pottery Barn and J. Crew has given some blocks the feeling of an outdoor suburban shopping mall.

Sights to See

Numbers in the margin correspond to points of interest on the SoHo, Little Italy, and Chinatown map.

Children's Museum of the Arts. In a loftlike space in SoHo, children ages 1 to 10 have the chance to become actively involved in visual and performing arts. They can play with brightly colored balls, draw on a computer, read in a special corner, and have fun in an art workshop. ⊠ *72 Spring St.,* ☏ *212/941–9198.* ☞ *$4 weekdays, $5 weekends.* ☉ *Tues.–Fri. noon–6, weekends 11–5.*

Greene Street. Cast-iron architecture is at its finest here; the block between Canal and Grand streets (⊠ 8–34 Greene St.) represents the longest row of cast-iron buildings anywhere. Handsome as they are, these buildings were always commercial. Notice the iron loading docks and the sidewalk vault covers that lead into basement storage areas. Two standout buildings on Greene Street are the so-called **Queen of Green Street** (⊠ 28–30 Greene St.), whose dormers, columns, window arches, projecting central bays, and Second Empire roof have a grace that is indeed regal; and its more masculine counterpart, **King of Greene Street** (⊠ 72–76 Greene St.), two blocks north, with a magnificent projecting porch of Corinthian columns and pilasters. Today the King (now painted ivory) houses the M-13 art gallery, Alice's Antiques, and Bennison Fabrics.

Guggenheim Museum SoHo. Since it opened in 1992, this downtown branch of the uptown museum has displayed a revolving series of exhibitions, both contemporary work and pieces from the Guggenheim's permanent collection. The

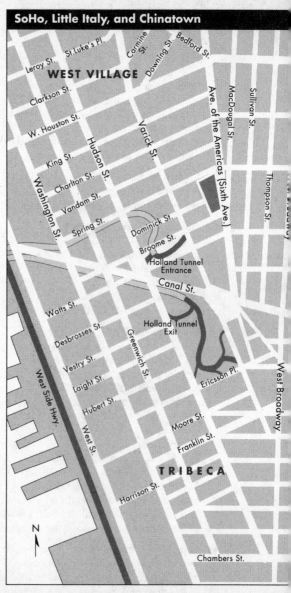

SoHo, Little Italy, and Chinatown

WEST VILLAGE

Leroy St.

St. Luke's Pl.

Carmine St.

Downing St.

Bedford St.

Clarkson St.

W. Houston St.

King St.

Charlton St.

Vandam St.

Spring St.

Washington St.

Hudson St.

Varick St.

Ave. of the Americas (Sixth Ave.)

MacDougal St.

Sullivan St.

Thompson St.

Dominick St.

Broome St.

Holland Tunnel Entrance

Canal St.

Watts St.

Desbrosses St.

Vestry St.

Laight St.

Hubert St.

Greenwich St.

Holland Tunnel Exit

Ericsson Pl.

West Broadway

West Side Hwy.

West St.

Moore St.

Franklin St.

TRIBECA

Harrison St.

N

Chambers St.

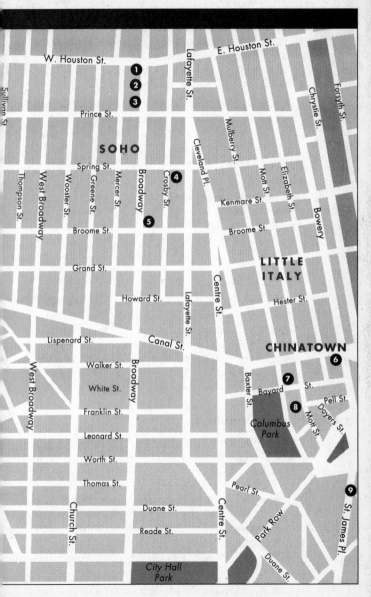

museum occupies space in a landmark 19th-century red-brick structure with its original cast-iron storefronts and detailed cornice. Arata Isozaki designed the two floors of stark, loftlike galleries as well as the museum store facing Broadway. ⊠ *575 Broadway, at Prince St.,* ☎ *212/423–3500.* ▣ *$6.* ☉ *Wed.–Fri. and Sun. 11–6, Sat. 11–8.*

 Haughwout Building. Nicknamed the Parthenon of Cast Iron, this Venetian-palazzo-style structure was built in 1857 to house Eder Haughwout's china and glassware business. Inside, the building once contained the world's first commercial passenger elevator, a steam-powered device invented by Elisha Graves Otis. ⊠ *488 Broadway, at Broome St.*

❶ Museum for African Art. Dedicated to contemporary and traditional African art, this small but expertly conceived museum is housed in a handsome two-story space designed by Maya Lin, who also designed the Vietnam Veterans Memorial in Washington, D.C. Exhibits may include contemporary sculpture, ceremonial masks, architectural details, costumes, and textiles. ⊠ *593 Broadway, near Houston St.,* ☎ *212/966–1313.* ▣ *$4.* ☉ *Tues.–Fri. 10:30–5:30, weekends noon–6.*

❷ New Museum of Contemporary Art. The avant-garde exhibitions here, all by living artists, are often radically innovative and socially conscious. ⊠ *583 Broadway, between Houston and Prince Sts.,* ☎ *212/219–1222.* ▣ *$4; free Sat. 6 PM–8 PM.* ☉ *Wed.–Fri. and Sun. noon–6, Sat. noon–8.*

Little Italy and Chinatown

Mulberry Street is the heart of Little Italy; in fact, at this point it's virtually the entire body. In 1932 an estimated 98% of the inhabitants of this area were of Italian birth or heritage, but since then the growth and expansion of neighboring Chinatown have encroached on the Italian neighborhood to such an extent that merchants and community leaders of the Little Italy Restoration Association (LIRA) negotiated a truce in which it was agreed that at least Mulberry would remain an all-Italian street.

In the second half of the 19th century, when Italian immigration peaked, the neighborhood stretched from Houston

Street to Canal Street and the Bowery to Broadway. During this time Italians founded at least three Italian parishes, including the Church of the Transfiguration (now almost wholly Chinese); they also operated an Italian-language newspaper, *Il Progresso*. In 1926 immigrants from southern Italy celebrated the first Feast of San Gennaro along Mulberry Street—a 10-day street fair that still takes place every September. Dedicated to the patron saint of Naples, the festival transforms Mulberry Street into a virtual alfresco restaurant, as wall-to-wall vendors sell traditional fried sausages and pastries. Today the festival is one of the few reminders of Little Italy's vibrant history, as the neighborhood continues to be overwhelmed by the ever-expanding Chinatown and as Italians continue to move out of Manhattan. Still, the neighborhood is full of enticing eateries and historical sights of interest.

Visibly exotic, Chinatown is a popular tourist attraction, but it is also a real, vital community where about half of the city's population of 300,000 Chinese still live. Its main businesses are restaurants and garment factories; some 55% of its residents speak little or no English. Theoretically, Chinatown is divided from Little Italy by Canal Street. However, in recent years an influx of immigrants from the People's Republic of China, Taiwan, and especially Hong Kong has swelled Manhattan's Chinese population, and Hong Kong residents, anticipating the return of the British colony to PRC domination in 1997, have been investing their capital in Chinatown real estate. Consequently, Chinatown now spills over its traditional borders into Little Italy to the north and the formerly Jewish Lower East Side to the east.

The first Chinese immigrants were primarily railroad workers who came from the West in the 1870s to settle in a limited section of the Lower East Side. For nearly a century, anti-immigration laws prohibited most men from having their wives and families join them; the neighborhood became known as a "bachelor society," and for years its population remained static. It was not until the end of World War II, when Chinese immigration quotas were increased, that the neighborhood began the outward expansion that is still taking place today. As a result of its rapid growth,

Chinatown has become more lively than ever. Where once there was just a handful of businesses in Chinatown, today it's a virtual marketplace, crammed with souvenir shops and restaurants in colorful pagoda-style buildings and crowded with pedestrians day and night.

Sights to See

Numbers in the margin correspond to points of interest on the SoHo, Little Italy, and Chinatown map.

6 Asian American Arts Centre. This place may look plain, but it does offer impressive contemporary works by Asian-American artists and annual Chinese folk-art exhibitions during the Chinese New Year. There's no sign out front and the door reads "KTV-City"; ring buzzer No. 1. ⊠ *26 Bowery, between Bayard and Canal Sts.,* ☎ *212/233–2154.* 🖃 *Free.* ☉ *Tues.–Fri. noon–6, Sat. 3–6.*

8 Church of the Transfiguration. Built in 1801 as the Zion Episcopal Church, this is an imposing Georgian structure with Gothic windows. It is now a Chinese Catholic church distinguished by its trilingualism: Here Mass is said in Cantonese, Mandarin, and English. ⊠ *25 Mott St.,* ☎ *212/962–5157.*

Doyers Street. The "bloody angle"—an unexpected sharp turn halfway down this little alleyway—was the site of turn-of-the-century battles between Chinatown's Hip Sing and On Leon tongs, gangs who fought for control over the local gambling and opium trades. Today the street is among the most colorful in Chinatown, lined with tea parlors and barbershops.

9 First Shearith Israel Graveyard. Consecrated in 1656 by the country's oldest Jewish congregation, this small burial ground bears the remains of Sephardic Jews (of Spanish-Portuguese extraction) who emigrated from Brazil in the mid-17th century. ⊠ *55 St. James Pl.*

Mulberry Street. Crowded with restaurants, cafés, bakeries, imported-food shops, and souvenir stores, Mulberry Street is where Little Italy lives and breathes. Especially on weekends, this is a street for strolling, gawking, and inhaling the aroma of garlic and olive oil.

Museum of Chinese in the Americas (MCA). In a century-old schoolhouse that once served Italian-American and Chinese-American children, MCA is the only U.S. museum devoted to preserving the history of the Chinese people throughout the Western Hemisphere. A gallery designed by Billie Tsien enhances the museum. The permanent exhibit entitled "Where's Home? Chinese in the Americas" explores the Chinese-American experience by weaving together displays of artists' creations and personal and domestic artifacts with historical documentation. Changing exhibits fill a second room; recent shows dealt with sights around Chinatown and Brooklyn's Sunset Park Chinese community. An archives dedicated to Chinese-American history and culture includes 2,000 volumes; it's open by appointment only. ⊠ *70 Mulberry St., 2nd floor,* ☎ *212/619–4785.* ☒ *$3.* ☉ *Tues.–Sun. 10:30–5.*

Lower Manhattan

Island city that it is, much of Manhattan strangely turns its back on the rushing waters that surround it. Not so the Battery. From waterside walks in Battery Park, you can look out on the confluence of the Hudson and East River estuaries where bustling commerce once glutted the harbor that built the "good city of old Manhatto," Herman Melville's moniker from the second chapter of *Moby-Dick*.

It was here that the Dutch established the colony of Nieuw Amsterdam in 1625; in 1789 the first capital building of the United States found itself here. The city did not really expand beyond these precincts until the middle of the 19th century. Today this historic heart of New York is increasingly being abandoned by companies for cheaper and better-equipped buildings in midtown and the suburbs, but all sorts of tax breaks, rezonings, and incentives, including plans to convert parts of some buildings to residences, are being worked up to help the area maintain its vitality. Lower Manhattan is still in many ways dominated by Wall Street, which is both an actual street and a shorthand name for the vast, powerful financial community that clusters around the New York and American stock exchanges.

The South Street Seaport restoration, centered on Fulton Street between Water Street and the East River, preserves the era of the clipper ship during the 19th century, when New York was a major seaport. Only a few blocks away, you can visit another seat of New York history—the City Hall neighborhood—and just north, spanning the East River, is that formidable testament to 19th-century engineering ingenuity, the Brooklyn Bridge.

Sights to See

Numbers in the margin correspond to points of interest on the Lower Manhattan map.

❶ Battery Park. This verdant landfill is loaded with monuments. The park's name refers to a line of cannons once mounted here to defend the shoreline (which ran along what is currently State Street). Starting near the Staten Island Ferry Terminal, head north along the water's edge to the **East Coast Memorial,** a statue of a fierce eagle that presides over eight granite slabs inscribed with the names of U.S. servicemen who died in the western Atlantic during World War II. Climb the steps of the East Coast Memorial for a fine view of the main features of **New York Harbor;** from left to right: **Governors Island,** a Coast Guard installation that is looking for a new tenant for 1998 and beyond, when the Coast Guard will leave it; hilly **Staten Island** in the distance; the **Statue of Liberty** on Liberty Island; **Ellis Island,** gateway to the New World for generations of immigrants; and the old railway terminal in **Liberty State Park,** on the mainland in Jersey City, New Jersey.

Continue north past a romantic **statue of Giovanni da Verrazano,** the Florentine merchant who piloted the ship that first sighted New York and its harbor in 1524. The **Verrazano-Narrows Bridge** between Brooklyn and Staten Island is visible from here, just beyond Governors Island.

Bowling Green. This oval greensward at the foot of Broadway became New York's first public park in 1733. On July 9, 1776, a few hours after citizens learned about the signing of the Declaration of Independence, rioters toppled a statue of British king George III that had occupied the spot for 11 years; much of the statue's lead was melted down into bullets. In 1783, when the occupying British forces fled the city, they defiantly hoisted a Union Jack on a greased, uncleated flagpole so it couldn't be lowered; patriot John Van Arsdale drove his own cleats into the pole to replace the flag with the Stars and Stripes.

★ ⑮ **Brooklyn Bridge.** Before this bridge was built, Brooklynites had to rely on the Fulton Street ferry to get to Brooklyn—a charming way to travel, surely, but unreliable in fog or ice. After some 50 years of talk about a bridge, John Augustus Roebling, a respected engineer, was handed a construction assignment in 1867. (Ironically, he was fatally injured by a ferry in 1869.) As the project to build the first steel suspension bridge slowly took shape over the next 15 years, it captured the imagination of the city; on its completion in 1883, it was called the Eighth Wonder of the World. It is hardly the longest suspension bridge in the world anymore, but it remains a symbol of human accomplishment. As you look south from the walkway, the pinnacles of downtown Manhattan loom on your right, Brooklyn Heights rises on your left, Governor's Island is washed by the tides, and the harbor opens toward Lady Liberty, showing herself in profile. You'd do well to bring a hat or scarf to protect you during the half hour it take to cross the bridge, as the wind can whip through the cables like a dervish.

❷ **Castle Clinton.** In Battery Park, this circular red-stone fortress first stood on an island 200 ft from shore as a defense for New York Harbor. In 1824 it became Castle Garden, an entertainment and concert facility that reached its zenith in 1850 when more than 6,000 people (the capacity of Radio City Music Hall) attended the U.S. debut of the Swedish Nightingale, Jenny Lind. After landfill connected it to the city, Castle Clinton became, in succession, an immigrant processing center, an aquarium, and now a restored fort, museum, and ticket office for ferries to the ☞ **Statue of Liberty** and ☞ **Ellis Island.** The ferry ride is one loop; you can get off at Liberty Island, visit the statue, then reboard any ferry and continue on to Ellis Island, boarding another boat once you have finished exploring the historic immigration facility there. *Castle Clinton:* ☎ *212/269–5755.* ⊙ *Tours hourly 10:35–3:35 daily. Ferry information:* ☎ *212/269–5755;* ✉ *$7 round-trip;* ⊙ *Departures daily every 30 mins 9:30–3:30 (more departures and extended hrs in summer).*

52

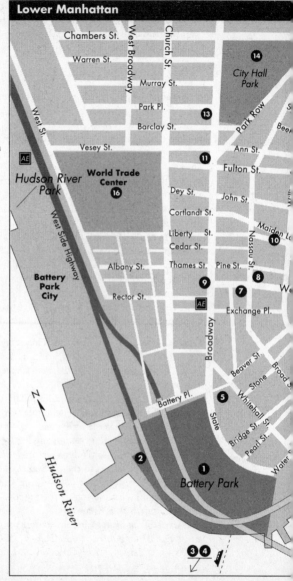

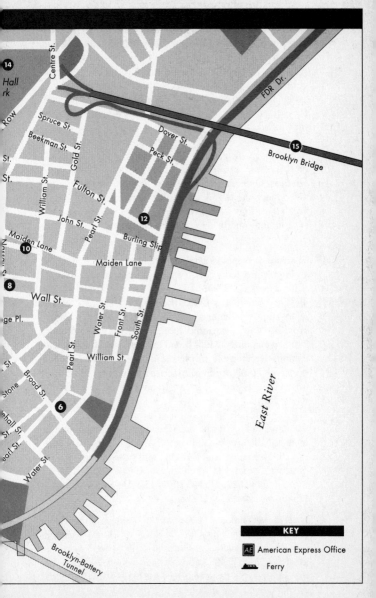

KEY

AE American Express Office

Ferry

⑭ City Hall. For a city as overwhelming as New York, this main government building, built between 1803 and 1812, is unexpectedly decorous. Originally its front and sides were clad in white marble while the back was faced in cheap brownstone, because city fathers assumed New York would never grow farther north than this. Limestone now covers all four sides. The Governor's Room at the head of the stairs, used for ceremonial events, is filled with historic portraits and furniture, including a writing table that George Washington used in 1789 when New York was the U.S. capital. The blue room, which was traditionally the mayor's office, is on the ground floor; it is now used for mayoral press conferences. On either side of the edifice are free interactive video machines that dispense information/propaganda on area attractions, civic procedures, City Hall history, mass transit, and other topics. ⊠ *City Hall Park,* ☏ *212/788–6879 for tour information.*

★ ④ Ellis Island. Approximately 17 million men, women, and children entered the country at this federal immigration facility between 1892 and 1954—the ancestors of more than 40% of Americans living today. After a $140 million restoration, the center opened in September 1990 to record crowds. Now a national monument, the island's main building contains the **Ellis Island Immigration Museum,** with exhibits detailing not only the island's history but the whole history of immigration to America. Perhaps the most moving exhibit is the American Immigrant Wall of Honor, where the names of nearly 400,000 immigrant Americans are inscribed along an outdoor promenade overlooking the Statue of Liberty and the Manhattan skyline. The names include Miles Standish, Priscilla Alden, George Washington's grandfather, Irving Berlin, and possibly an ancestor of yours. For ferry information, *see* Castle Clinton, *above. Ellis Island:* ☏ *212/363–3200; 212/883–1986 for Wall of Honor information.* ☒ *Free.*

⑧ Federal Hall National Memorial. On the steps of this Greek Revival building stands a regal statue of George Washington, who on that site was sworn in as the nation's first president in 1789. The likeness was made by noted sculptor and presidential relative John Quincy Adams Ward. After the capital moved to Philadelphia in 1790, the original Federal

Hall became New York's City Hall, then was demolished in 1812 when the present City Hall (☞ *above*) was completed. The clean and simple lines of the current structure, built as a U.S. Customs House in 1842, were modeled on the Parthenon, a potent symbol for a young nation striving to emulate classic Greek democracy. It's now a museum featuring exhibits on New York and Wall Street. ⊠ *26 Wall St.,* ☎ *212/825–6888.* 🎟 *Free.* ☉ *Weekdays 9–5, and weekends in summer 9–5.*

⑩ Federal Reserve Bank. Gray, solid, imposing, and absolutely impregnable, this is how a bank should look. Built in 1935, this neo-Renaissance structure made of sandstone, limestone, and ironwork goes five levels underground. Vaults here reputedly contain a third of the world's gold reserves. The bank was the setting for a robbery scene in the movie *Die Hard II.* ⊠ *33 Liberty St.,* ☎ *212/720–6130.* 🎟 *Free.* ☉ *1-hr tour by advance (at least 5 days) reservation, weekdays at 10:30, 11:30, 1:30, and 2:30.*

⑥ Fraunces Tavern. The main building is a stately Colonial house with a white marble portico and coffered frieze, built in 1719 and converted to a tavern in 1762. It was the meeting place for the Sons of Liberty up until the Revolutionary War. This was also the site where, in 1783, George Washington delivered a farewell address to his officers celebrating the British evacuation of New York. Later, the building housed some offices of the fledgling U.S. government. Today, a museum, restaurant, and bar compose this historic five-building complex. ⊠ *54 Pearl St., at Broad St.,* ☎ *212/425–1778.* 🎟 *Museum $2.50.* ☉ *Museum weekdays 10–4:45, weekends noon–4.*

★ ⑤ National Museum of the American Indian. This museum is the first of its kind to be dedicated to Native American culture, with well-mounted exhibits that examine the history and the current cultures of native peoples from all over the Americas through literature, dance, lectures, readings, film, and crafts. The museum is housed in an ornate Beaux Arts (1907) gem that originally functioned as the **Alexander Hamilton Custom House.** George Gustav Heye, a wealthy New Yorker, amassed most of the museum's collection, which includes pottery, weaving, and basketry from the southwestern United States, painted hides from the Plains Indians of North America, carved jade from the Mexican Olmec and Maya cultures, and contemporary Native American paintings. There is a research library, a media room with interactive computer programs, and a gift shop off the main lobby. ⊠ *1 Bowling Green,* ☎ *212/668–6624.* ⊡ *Free.* ☉ *Daily 10–5, Thurs. 10–8.*

❼ New York Stock Exchange. The stock exchange nearly bursts from this little building, constructed before modern technology came to Wall Street. After what may be a lengthy wait, you can take an elevator to the third-floor visitor center. A self-guided tour, informative slide shows, video displays, and guides may help you interpret the seeming chaos you'll see from the visitors' gallery overlooking the immense (50-ft-high) trading hall. ⊠ *Tickets available at 20 Broad St.,* ☎ *212/656–5165.* ⊡ *Free tickets distributed beginning at 9; come before 1 PM to assure entrance.* ☉ *Weekdays 9:15–4.*

★ Robert F. Wagner Jr. Park. The link in the chain of parks that stretches from Battery Park to above the World Financial Center, this newest addition to the downtown waterfront may be the best of the bunch. Lawns, walks, gardens, and benches spill right down to the river. Behind these, a brownbrick structure rises two stories to provide river and harbor panoramas. ⊠ *Between Battery Pl. and the Hudson River.*

⓫ St. Paul's Chapel. The oldest (1766) surviving church in Manhattan, this Episcopal house of worship was the site of the prayer service following George Washington's inauguration as president. Built of rough Manhattan brownstone, it was modeled on London's St. Martin-in-the-Fields. It's open until 3 every day except Saturday for prayer and meditation; look in the north aisle for Washington's pew. ⊠ *Broadway and Fulton St.,* ☎ *212/602–0874.*

★ ⓬ South Street Seaport Historic District. Had it not been declared a historic district in 1967, this charming, cobblestone corner of the city would likely have been gobbled up by skyscrapers. The Rouse Corporation, which had already created slick so-called festival marketplaces in Boston (Quincy Market) and Baltimore (Harborplace), was hired to restore and adapt the existing historic buildings, preserving the commercial feel of centuries past. On the south side of Fulton Street is the seaport's architectural centerpiece, **Schermerhorn Row,** a redbrick terrace of Georgian- and Federal-style warehouses and countinghouses built in 1811–12. Today the ground floors are occupied by upscale shops, bars, and restaurants, and the **South Street Seaport Museum.** ✉ *12 Fulton St.,* ☎ *212/669–9400; 212/732–7678 for events and shopping information.* ✇ *$6 (to ships, galleries, walking tours, Maritime Crafts Center, films, and other seaport events).* ☉ *Museum Apr.–Sept., daily 10–6, Thurs. 10–8; Oct.–Mar., Wed.–Mon. 10–5.*

★ ❸ **Statue of Liberty.** After arriving on Liberty Island (*see* Castle Clinton, *above,* for ferry information), you have two ways to get from the ground-floor entrance to the monument: You can take an elevator 10 stories to the top of the 89-ft-high pedestal, or if you're strong of heart and limb, you can climb 354 steps (the equivalent of a 22-story building) to the crown. (Visitors cannot go up into the torch.) It usually takes two to three hours to walk up to the crown because of the wait beforehand. Erected in 1886 and refurbished for its centennial, the Statue of Liberty weighs 225 tons and stands 151 ft from her feet to her torch. ✉ *Liberty Island,* ☎ *212/363–3200.* ✇ *Free.*

❾ **Trinity Church.** Established as an Anglican parish in 1697, the present structure (1846), by Richard Upjohn, ranked as the city's tallest building for most of the second half of the 19th century. Its three huge bronze doors were designed by Richard Morris Hunt to recall Lorenzo Ghiberti's doors for the Baptistery in Florence, Italy. After the exterior sandstone was restored in 1991, New Yorkers were amazed to discover that a church they had always thought of as black was actually rosy pink—now it's faded back to a sandy color. The church's Gothic Revival interior is surprisingly light and elegant. On the church's north side is a 2½-acre graveyard: Alexander Hamilton is buried beneath a white stone pyramid. ✉ *74 Trinity Pl. (Broadway at the head of Wall St.),* ☎ *212/602–0800.*

Wall Street. The street is named after a wood wall built across the island in 1653 to defend the Dutch colony against the

Native Americans. Arguably the most famous thorough-fare in the world, though only a third of a mile long, Wall Street began its financial career with stock traders conducting business along the sidewalks or at tables beneath a sheltering buttonwood tree. Today it's a dizzyingly narrow canyon—look to the east and you'll glimpse a sliver of East River waterfront, look to the west and you'll see the spire of Trinity Church, tightly framed by skyscrapers at the head of the street.

★ ⑬ **Woolworth Building.** Called the Cathedral of Commerce, this ornate white terra-cotta edifice was, at 792 ft, the world's tallest building when it opened in 1913; it still houses the Woolworth corporate offices. Take a peek at the **lobby:** Among its Gothic-style details are sculptures set into arches in the lobby ceiling; one of them represents an elderly F. W. Woolworth pinching his pennies, while another depicts the architect, Cass Gilbert, cradling in his arms a model of his creation. ⊠ *Park Pl. and Broadway.*

★ ✆ ⑯ **World Trade Center.** This 16-acre, 12-million-square-ft complex contains New York's two tallest buildings (each 1,350 ft high). To reach the **Top of the World** observation deck on the 107th floor of 2 World Trade Center, elevators glide a quarter of a mile into the sky—in only 58 seconds. The view potentially extends 55 mi, although signs at the ticket window disclose how far you can see that day and whether the outdoor deck is open. In February 1993, the Center was the site of a bombing by terrorists that killed six people and caused extensive damage to the area. However, the Center has, for the most part, returned to normal operations, though security has been tightened considerably within the complex. ☎ *212/323–2340.* ⊠ *$10.* ☉ *June–Aug., daily 9:30 AM–11:30 PM; Sept.–May, daily 9:30– 9:30.*

Off the Beaten Path

★ ✆ **Bronx Zoo.** Opened in 1899, this zoo is one of the nation's largest, with 265 acres and more than 4,000 animals representing more than 600 species. It's full of fascinating exhibits in naturalistic settings such as "Jungle World," an indoor tropical rain forest complete with five waterfalls, millipedes, flowering orchids, and pythons; "Wild Asia," where tigers and elephants roam free on nearly 40 acres of open meadows and dark forests; and "World of Birds," a huge, glassed-in aviary. Three different rides, including a shuttle bus, a monorail, and a tram, offer various perspectives of the grounds during summer. The **Children's Zoo** has many hands-on learning activities, as well as a large petting zoo. At the **Zoo Center,** visitors will find a rare black rhino. To get to the Bronx Zoo, take Subway 2 to Pelham Parkway and walk three blocks west; or catch the Liberty Line Bx M11 express bus (☎ 718/652–8400) from mid-Manhattan. ⊠ *Bronx River Pkwy. and Fordham Rd.,* ☎ *718/367–1010.* ☞ *Apr.–Oct., Thurs.–Tues. $6.75; Nov.–Mar., Thurs.–Tues. $3; free Wed.* ۩ *Mar.–Oct., weekdays 10–5, weekends 10–5:30; Nov.–Feb., daily 10–4:30. Children's Zoo:* ☞ *$2;* ۩ *Apr.–Oct.*

★ ۞ **Brooklyn Botanic Garden.** A major attraction at this 52-acre botanic garden, one of the finest in the country, is the beguiling **Japanese Garden**—complete with a blazing red *torii* gate and a pond laid out in the shape of the Chinese character for "heart." You can also wander through the **Cranford Rose Garden** (5,000 bushes, 1,200 varieties); the **Fragrance Garden,** designed especially for the blind; the **Shakespeare Garden,** featuring more than 80 plants immortalized by the Bard; and **Celebrity Path,** Brooklyn's answer to Hollywood's Walk of Fame, with the names of homegrown stars inscribed on stepping-stones. A complex of handsome greenhouses called the **Steinhardt Conservatory** holds thriving desert, tropical, temperate, and aquatic vegetation. The extraordinary **C.V. Starr Bonsai Museum** in the conservatory exhibits about 80 miniature Japanese specimens. Free tours are given weekends at 1 PM, except for holiday weekends. ⊠ *1000 Washington Ave., between Empire Blvd. and south side of Brooklyn Museum,* ☎ *718/622–4433.* ☞ *$3; free Tues.* ۩ *Garden Apr.–Sept., Tues.–Fri. 8–6, weekends 10–6; Oct.–Mar., Tues.–Fri. 8–4:30, weekends 10–4:30. Steinhardt Conservatory Apr.–Sept., Tues.–Sun. 10–5:30; Oct.–Mar., Tues.–Sun. 10–4.*

★ **Brooklyn Heights Promenade.** East–west streets—from Orange on the north to Remsen on the south—end at this ⅓-mi-long sliver of park, which hangs over Brooklyn's industrial waterfront like one of Babylon's fabled gardens. Cantilevered over two lanes of the Brooklyn–Queens Expressway and a service road, the esplanade has benches offering some of the most enthralling views anywhere of the Manhattan skyline.

The Cloisters. Perched atop a wooded hill near Manhattan's northernmost tip, the Cloisters houses the Metropolitan Museum of Art's medieval European collection in the style of a medieval monastery. Colonnaded walks connect authentic French and Spanish monastic cloisters, a French Romanesque chapel, a 12th-century chapter house, and a Romanesque apse. An entire room is devoted to a superb set of 15th- and 16th-century tapestries depicting a unicorn hunt. The view of the Hudson River and the New Jersey Palisades (an undeveloped Rockefeller family preserve) enhances the experience. From Harlem, the Cloisters is easily accessible by public transportation. The M4 "Cloisters–Fort Tryon Park" bus provides a lengthy but scenic ride; catch it along Broadway, or take Subway A to 190th Street. If you're traveling from below 110th Street, Bus M4 runs along Madison Avenue. ⊠ *Fort Tryon Park,* ☎ *212/923–3700.* ☎ *$8 (suggested donation).* ⊙ *Tues.–Sun. 9:30–5:15; closes at 4:45 Nov.–Feb.*

★ **New York Botanical Garden.** Considered one of the leading botany centers of the world, this 250-acre garden built around the dramatic gorge of the Bronx River is one of the best reasons to make a trip to the Bronx. The garden was founded by Dr. Nathaniel Lord Britton and his wife, Elizabeth. After visiting England's Kew Gardens in 1889, they returned full of fervor to create a similar haven in New York. In 1991 the New York Botanical Garden celebrated its centennial. A walk along the Bronx River from the mill leads the visitor to the garden's 40-acre **Forest,** the largest remnant of the forest that once covered New York City. Outdoor plant collections include the **Peggy Rockefeller Rose Garden,** with 230 different kinds of roses. At the **Museum Building** there's a gardening shop, a library, and a world-renowned herbarium with 6 million dried plant specimens.

With the completion of a four-year renovation in 1997, the historic **Enid A. Haupt Conservatory** once again displays rain forests, deserts, and special exhibitions. An even newer attraction is the **Everett Children's Adventure Garden,** 8 acres of plant and science exhibits for children, including a boulder maze, giant animal topiaries, a wild wetland trail, and a plant discovery center. To get to the Botanical Garden, take the Metro North train (☎ 212/532–4900) to the garden from Grand Central Terminal; or take Subway D or 4 to the Bedford Park Boulevard stop and walk eight blocks east to the entrance on Bedford Park Boulevard. ⊠ *200th St. and Southern Blvd.,* ☎ *718/817–8700.* ⌷ *$3; free Sat. 10–noon and Wed. Parking $4.* ☉ *Nov.–Mar., Tues.–Sun. 10–4; Apr.–Oct., Tues.–Sun. 10–6.*

3 Dining

By J. Walman

IN MOST GREAT RESTAURANT TOWNS, there is generally one best restaurant; New York generously offers a variety of candidates. Times being what they are, top restaurants have short lives, chefs play musical kitchens, and today's star is often tomorrow's laggard. So temper your visits to famous restaurants with informed selections from among lesser-knowns.

When it comes to cost, New York gets a bum rap. Of course, you can order caviar and champagne or Bordeaux of great years; you will pay accordingly. But you will also do that in Nashville, Chicago, and Los Angeles. Our point is that each price stratum has its own equilibrium. Translation: $20 is only inexpensive if you get $20 worth of value, and $100 may be a bargain.

If you're watching your budget, always ask the price of the specials, which have become a way for restaurants to charge higher-than-normal prices. Rather than being sensibly attached to the menu, European-style, specials are often recited by the waiter with no mention of cost. Also consider ordering two or more appetizers in lieu of entrées and sharing, since appetizers are often generous in size and more interesting than more conventional entrées. Finally, always go over your bill. Mistakes do occur (and not always in the restaurant's favor).

Make a reservation. If you change your mind, cancel—it's only courteous. Tables can be hard to come by between 7 and 9; if a restaurant tells you that it can seat you only before 6 or after 10, you may decide that it doesn't need you. Or you may be persuaded that eating early or late is okay. Eating after a play or concert is quite common in New York, and there's no shortage of options.

CATEGORY	COST*
$$$$	over $60
$$$	$40–$59
$$	$20–$39
$	under $20

*per person for a three-course meal, excluding drinks, service, and 8¼% sales tax

Lower Manhattan

CONTEMPORARY

$$$–$$$$ ✕ **Hudson River Club.** This distinguished restaurant has spacious wood-paneled rooms with paisley-print banquettes, spectacular views of the Hudson River and the Statue of Liberty, and a spirited bar with piano music. The kitchen celebrates Hudson River valley produce in such hallmark dishes as mint-cured, apple-smoked salmon Napoleon and veal shank with horseradish mashed potatoes. Desserts—like the signature tower of chocolate (combining brownie, mousse, and meringue)—are edible sculptures, while the New York State cheese plate with walnut bread and nut muffins serves as a perfect foil to the magnificent wines from the regional American wine list. ⊠ *4 World Financial Center,* ☎ *212/786–1500. Reservations essential. AE, DC, MC, V. No lunch Sat.*

$$$–$$$$ ✕ **Windows on the World.** This monumental restaurant on
★ the World Trade Center's 107th floor reopened in 1996 after a $25 million makeover. The complex now includes The Greatest Bar on Earth (actually three bars) with a full, multiethnic menu and dancing after 10 PM; the adjacent Skybox, a cigar-smoking oasis; and the intimate, 60-seat Cellar in the Sky, where a seven-course dinner is served, accompanied by five wines. The 240-seat main dining room has artwork by Milton Glaser, apricot-fabric banquettes, origami fabric-wrapped ceilings, and panoramic windows with stunning Manhattan views. Don't miss the whole seared foie gras, roasted in Sauternes and grapes, served with a galette of pear and potatoes. Follow this with a whole veal shank, roasted with cumin, garlic, and Mexican aromatics. ⊠ *1 World Trade Center, 107th floor,* ☎ *212/524–7011; 212/938–0030 for Cellar in the Sky. Reservations essential. Jacket required. AE, DC, MC, V.*

SoHo and TriBeCa

CONTEMPORARY

$$$$ ✕ **Chanterelle.** Soft peach walls, luxuriously spaced ta-
★ bles, towering ceilings, and glorious displays of flowers set the stage for what is arguably New York's finest new-American restaurant. Although the signature seafood

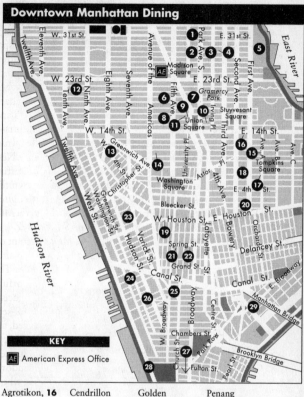

Downtown Manhattan Dining

KEY

AE American Express Office

sausage, charred on the outside and succulent within, and the Japanese-style raw seafood are both always available, other dishes on the menu are dictated by the bounty of the seasons. Lunch and dinner are prix fixe. ⊠ *2 Harrison St., near Hudson St.,* ☎ *212/966–6960. Reservations essential. AE, DC, MC, V. Closed Sun.–Mon. No lunch.*

FRENCH

\$\$–\$\$\$ ✕ **Capsouto Frères.** You'd never guess this romantic spot
★ with exposed brick walls, tall columns, and wooden floors was once a warehouse. With its top-notch service, classical music, and reasonable prices, this 1891 TriBeCa landmark is also a winner. The terrine Provençale and Peking duck in cassis-ginger sauce are classics. Dessert soufflés around town pale against the light, delicious versions here. ⊠ *451 Washington St., near Watts St.,* ☎ *212/966–4900. Reservations essential. AE, DC, MC, V. No lunch Mon.*

JAPANESE

\$\$\$–\$\$\$\$ ✕ **Nobu.** A curved wall of river-worn black pebbles, a 12-
★ seat onyx-faced sushi bar (perfect for single diners), bare-wood tables, birch trees, and a hand-painted beech floor create drama. It's difficult to decide which direction to go on the menu: rock-shrimp tempura; black cod with miso; new-style sashimi—all are tours de force. ⊠ *105 Hudson St., off Franklin St.,* ☎ *212/219–0500 or 212/219–8095 for same-day reservations. Reservations essential. AE, DC, MC, V. Closed Sun. No lunch.*

MALAYSIAN

\$–\$\$ ✕ **Penang SoHo.** This is a Technicolor fantasy, with a dramatic waterfall, palm trees, tropical flowers, bar seats with backs made of hoe handles, and individual little huts for small groups. The menu includes relatively authentic culinary masterpieces, such as *sarang burung,* a ring of fried taro filled with scallops, squid, shrimp, and vegetables. For dessert have a pancake filled with ground peanuts and sweet corn and an iced Malaysian coffee. ⊠ *109 Spring St., between Greene and Mercer Sts.,* ☎ *212/274–8883. AE, MC, V.*

PHILIPPINE

$$–$$$ ✕ **Cendrillon Asian Grill and Marimba Bar.** Cendrillon
★ means Cinderella in French, so the slipper-shape bar is apro-
pos. The all-exposed redbrick dining room has beautiful wood
tables with delicate inlay designs. Don't miss the spring
rolls, Asian barbecues (duck, spareribs, chicken), black rice
salad, and adobo—the national dish of the Philippines, prepared here with quail and rabbit in the traditional vinegar
and garlic sauce. ⊠ *45 Mercer St., between Broome and
Grand Sts.,* ☎ *212/343–9012. AE, DC, MC, V. Closed Sun.*

Chinatown, Little Italy, East Village

AMERICAN

$–$$ ✕ **First.** Come here for inner-city flavor, late-night dining,
and intriguing food. The decor features an open kitchen, ham-
mered-metal tables against silk horseshoe-shape banquettes,
and a bar graced with a lovely display of photographs by
local photographers. The wine list is carefully chosen (several fine vintages are available by the glass). On Sunday,
there's a fun brunch and a one-of-a-kind roast suckling pig
dinner. ⊠ *87 1st Ave., between 5th and 6th Sts.,* ☎ *212/674–
3823. Reservations essential. AE, MC, V. No lunch.*

CHINESE

$$ ✕ **Golden Unicorn.** This Hong Kong–style restaurant has
an outstanding 12-course banquet (which must be ordered
three days in advance), a real bargain if shared by 10.
Served in a small private room, it may include such dishes
as roast suckling pig, scallops and seafood in a noodle
nest, whole steamed fish, fried rice with raisins, lobster with
ginger, and unusual desserts based on warm or chilled fruit
or rice soups. If you're seeking something less elaborate,
sit in the regular dining room and order à la carte. ⊠ *18
E. Broadway, at Catherine St.,* ☎ *212/941–0911. AE,
MC, V.*

GREEK

$–$$ ✕ **Agrotikon.** Designed by artist Anna Lascari, this im-
★ maculate white, blue, and green dining room with two
fireplaces has been whimsically decorated with decals of fruit

and tiny blue fish. Owner and executive chef Kostis Tsingas oversees the most inventive Greek restaurant in town. Don't miss the meatballs of baby calamari. Also worth your while is the whole red snapper, accompanied by delightfully crunchy dandelion greens. ⊠ *322 E. 14th St., between 1st and 2nd Aves.,* ☎ *212/473–2602. AE, DC, MC, V. Closed Mon.*

LATIN

$ ✕ **Boca Chica.** At this raffish East Villager start with a po
★ tent *caipirinha* (Brazilian rum, lime juice, and sugar). Assertively seasoned food from several Latin American nations at giveaway prices is Boca Chica's forte. Check out the plantains, served as croquettes or filled with spicy meat; soupy Puerto Rican chicken-rice stew; or Cuban sandwiches blending roast pork, ham, and pickles. Lively music and dancing have their way on weekends, and watch your step—there's often an equally lively boa constrictor by the bar. ⊠ *13 1st Ave., near 1st St.,* ☎ *212/473–0108. AE, DC, MC, V. No lunch Mon.–Sat.*

SPANISH

$ ✕ **Xunta.** The dining room has wine barrels for tables, high stools (watch your balance), fish nets covering the ceiling, and a brick bar with overhanging dried peppers. Of the 32 tapas, don't miss the tortilla *española con cebola* (classic potato omelet with onions)—it is superb. Other recommended dishes include grilled shrimp, tuna or codfish empanadas, and sautéed *cigalas* (a typical shellfish in white wine and cherry-tomato sauce). ⊠ *174 1st Ave., between 10th and 11th Sts.,* ☎ *212/614–0620. AE, DC, MC, V.*

SWISS

$ ✕ **Roettelle A. G.** You'll love this charming East Village town
★ house where you can sit in a hidden nook in one of the several dining rooms, in the cozy bar, or under an arbor in the garden sipping Swiss wine and eating *viande de Grisons* (Swiss dried beef) or raclette (mild melted cheese served with boiled potatoes and tiny pickles). Sauerbraten with spaetzle and red cabbage is delicious, and it's rare to taste apple strudel and linzer torte this good. Prices are low, and there's also a bargain two-course fixed-price dinner. ⊠ *126 E. 7th St., between 1st Ave. and Ave. A,* ☎ *212/674–4140. Reservations essential. MC, V. Closed Sun.*

Greenwich Village

BARBECUE

$ ✕ Brothers Bar-B-Q. This huge, barnlike space on two levels has a lounge area decorated in the offbeat style of the American South. Monday night, it's all-you-can-eat; sample puffy hush puppies with hot sauce, smoked sausage over black-eyed peas, fried wings and smoked rib tips in bourbon sauce, shrimp po'boy sandwiches, and terrific chicken and ribs. There's enough of a selection of tequila shots to satisfy Pancho Villa, 11 bottled beers, and seven on tap. ⊠ *225 Varick St., at Clarkston St., ☎ 212/727–2775. AE.*

FRENCH

$–$$ ✕ L'Auberge Du Midi. If you want the "perfect Greenwich
★ Village restaurant," look no further than this seductive bistro, with its French country atmosphere combining exposed brick, copper pots, and stone floors. Try the unblemished roast rack of lamb with fresh thyme and *gratin chaud de pommes au Calvados* (glazed hot apples and almond paste, flavored with apple brandy). There's a charming sidewalk café, weather permitting. ⊠ *310 W. 4th St., between W. 12th and Bank Sts., ☎ 212/242–4705. Reservations essential. AE, MC, V. Closed Mon. Nov.–Mar. No lunch.*

$ ✕ French Roast. This casual, around-the-clock spot with a Left Bank ambience charges bargain prices for some very good bistro dishes rarely encountered, such as poached beef marrow finished with bread crumbs and served in broth. The *croque monsieur* (melted cheese sandwich, done in the style of French toast) is first-rate. Or just stop for coffee and dessert. ⊠ *458 6th Ave., at 11th St., ☎ 212/533–2233. AE, MC, V.*

PIZZA

$ ✕ Arturo's. Few guidebooks list this brick-walled Village landmark, but the body-to-body crowds teetering on the wobbly wooden chairs suggest good things. The pizza is terrific, cooked in a coal-fired oven. Basic pastas as well as seafood, veal, and chicken concoctions with mozzarella and lots of tomato sauce come at giveaway prices. ⊠ *106 W. Houston St., off Thompson St., ☎ 212/677–3820. AE, MC, V.*

Gramercy Park, Murray Hill, Chelsea

AMERICAN

$$$ ✕ **American Place.** This stylish establishment with kindly
★   service gets our vote as the country's finest regional American restaurant. The seasonal menu ranges from fresh Maine deviled-crab spring roll to cedar-planked salmon with seasonal vegetables. The high-ceilinged room with its Art Deco brasserie-style light fixtures, colorful Mikasa china, generously spaced tables, and Frank Stella paintings represents luxury at its most effortless. ⊠ *2 Park Ave., at 32nd St.,* ☎ *212/684–2122. Reservations essential. AE, DC, MC, V. No lunch weekends.*

$$ ✕ **Blue Water Grill.** This popular restaurant in what was
★   once a bank retains the original 1904 molded ceiling and marble. A copper-and-tile raw bar anchors one end of the sweeping room with its warm hues of indigo blue, sienna, and yellow. The menu is strong on seafood, served neat (chilled whole lobster; shrimp in the rough); in the au courant "global" style (Moroccan-spiced red snapper, Maryland crab cakes, warm shrimp cocktail in bamboo steamers with Japanese and Shanghai sauces); or in simple preparations from a wood-burning oven. ⊠ *31 Union Sq. W, at 16th St.,* ☎ *212/675–9500. Reservations essential. AE, DC, MC, V.*

$–$$ ✕ **Empire Diner.** This slick, chrome, '30s diner has starred in Madonna videos and Hollywood movies. Typical dinner fare with an upscale flare, such as hefty Portobello burgers, omelets with 18 fillings to choose from, and frothy root-beer floats, are best enjoyed in summer when there's outdoor seating and people-watching is at its prime. It's open 24 hours a day, seven days a week. ⊠ *210 10th Ave.,* ☎ *212/243–2736. AE, D, DC, MC, V.*

ASIAN

$–$$ ✕ **Republic.** This innovative Asian noodle emporium has two long bluestone bars at which you can simultaneously dine and enjoy the spectacle of chefs scurrying amid clouds of steam in the open kitchen. The menu contains chiefly rice dishes or noodles, stir-fried with hints of ginger, peanuts, and coriander or served in savory broths made with coconut milk, lemongrass, Asian basil, and lime leaf. There's also an uptown branch (⊠ *2290 Broadway, between 82nd and*

In case you want
to see the world.

At American Express, we're here to make your journey a
smooth one. So we have over 1,700 travel service locations
in over 120 countries ready to help. What else would you
expect from the world's largest travel agency?

do more

AMERICAN
EXPRESS

http://www.americanexpress.com/travel

Travel

In case you want to be welcomed there.

We're here to see that you're always welcomed at establishments everywhere. That's why millions of people carry the American Express® Card – for peace of mind, confidence, and security, around the world or just around the corner.

do more

AMERICAN EXPRESS

Cards

In case you're running low.

We're here to help with more than 118,000 Express Cash locations around the world. In order to enroll, just call American Express before you start your vacation.

do more

AMERICAN EXPRESS

Express Cash

And just in case.

We're here with American Express® Travelers Cheques
and Cheques *for Two*.® They're the safest way to carry
money on your vacation and the surest way to get a
refund, practically anywhere, anytime.
Another way we help you...

do more®

AMERICAN EXPRESS

Travelers Cheques

83rd Sts., ☎ 212/579–5959). ⊠ 37A Union Sq. W, between 16th and 17th Sts., ☎ 212/627–7172. AE, DC, MC, V.

CONTEMPORARY

$$$ ✕ **Water Club.** This glass-enclosed barge in the East River
★ is decidedly dramatic, with its long wood-paneled bar, blazing fireplace, appetizing shellfish display, and panoramic water views. Tuna tartare with marinated shiitake mushrooms, wasabi, spicy ocean salad, and flying-fish roe arrives on a porthole with a tiny anchor supporting a jar of caviar. Or order the exemplary sautéed red snapper fillet with lobster dumpling fennel and saffron bouillon. The flourless chocolate cake with peppermint-stick ice cream will sweeten even the sourest disposition. Sunday brunch is winsome. ⊠ 500 E. 30th St., ☎ 212/683–3333. Reservations essential. Jacket required. AE, DC, MC, V.

$$–$$$ ✕ **Flowers.** The intimate Tuscan-style dining room resem-
★ bles a country-barn interior. Baskets of dried flowers adorn the walls, and copper light-fixtures exude a comforting glow. The menu incorporates such influences as Asian (crispy shrimp roll with soy-ginger vinaigrette and spaghetti vegetables), Caribbean (roasted baby lamb chops with Jamaican spices), and Italian (risotto of seasonal wild mushrooms, asparagus, rosemary, and white truffle oil). Desserts are lovely—especially the baked Alaska. ⊠ 21 W. 17th St., between 5th and 6th Aves., ☎ 212/691–8888. AE, DC, MC, V. Closed Sun. No lunch Sat.

FRENCH

$$ ✕ **Les Halles.** Strikingly unpretentious, this French-Amer-
★ ican steak house has a homey interior, with posters plastered on antique walls, a tin ceiling, and a windowed kitchen. This is the place to go for crispy duck-leg confit and frisée salad, warm sausages with lentils, and heaping plates of garlicky cold cuts. A good bet is the extraordinary côte de boeuf with béarnaise sauce, a massive rib steak for two served from a wooden board. ⊠ 411 Park Ave. S, between 28th and 29th Sts., ☎ 212/679–4111. AE, DC, MC, V.

INDIAN

$–$$ ✕ **Mavalli Palace.** Service may be a bit slow here, but the gentle prices and marvelous dishes more than compensate. Magnificent crepes made with lentils and rice flour are wrapped around potatoes and a fiery chutney. Fresh onions top *uttappam,* a rice and lentil pancake. This pretty place has exposed brick walls and blond wood chairs. ⊠ *46 E. 29th St.,* ☎ *212/679–5535. AE, DC, MC, V. Closed Mon.*

LATIN

$$$ **✕ Patria.** This trendy trilevel Caribbean café, painted in strik-
★ ing earth tones, has handsome mosaics and an open grill. The fluctuating menu offers variations of several ethnic en- trées, such as meat, vegetable, or seafood empanadas, as well as soups and seafood (look for the crispy red snapper with coconut-conch rice). Even nonsmokers will want to indulge in the signature dessert, a chocolate cigar with ed- ible matches. ⊠ *250 Park Ave. S, at 20th St.,* ☎ *212/777– 6211. Reservations essential. AE, MC, V.*

SOUTHWESTERN

$$$ **✕ Mesa Grill.** Manhattan foodies flock to this former bank, now done up with vinyl banquettes, green-and-yellow walls, and industrial fans. You can't go wrong with the small menu. Try the shrimp with a roasted garlic and corn tamale, the pumpkin soup with chili cream, or the chili-crusted rab- bit with sweet-potato polenta and caramelized mango sauce. Chocolate–peanut butter ice cream cake with roasted marshmallows is just one of the unbeatable desserts. ⊠ *102 5th Ave., between 15th and 16th Sts.,* ☎ *212/807–7400. Reservations essential. AE, MC, V.*

TURKISH

$ **✕ Turkish Kitchen.** Manhattan's best Turkish restaurant is
★ housed in a striking multilevel room with lipstick-red walls, chairs with skirted slipcovers, framed prints, and kilims cov- ering the walls and floor. For appetizers, choose from such delectable offerings as velvety char-grilled eggplant salad, pan-fried calves' liver, and fried calamari. The stuffed cab- bage and bulgur-wheat patties, filled with ground lamb, pine nuts, and currants, are both highly recommended. ⊠ *386 3rd Ave., between 27th and 28th Sts.,* ☎ *212/679–1810. AE, DC, MC, V. No lunch weekends.*

VEGETARIAN

$–$$ **✕ Zen Palate.** In this remarkable vegetarian restaurant, walls are made from squares of fragile rice paper, and there are wooden beams and bamboo chairs. The resplendent appetizers include taro spring rolls, Vietnamese-style autumn rolls, and marinated seaweed. Entrées have poetic names like "Festival on a Roll" (seasoned spinach in soybean crepes with a spicy sauce) and "Dreamland" (layers of spinach linguine, bean sprouts, and shredded black mushrooms). ✉ *34 Union Sq. E, at 16th St.,* ☎ *212/614–9291;* ✉ *663 9th Ave.,* ☎ *212/582–1669;* ✉ *2170 Broadway,* ☎ *212/501–7768. AE, MC, V. No lunch Sun.*

Midtown

AFGHAN

$
★ ✕ **Pamir.** Afghan cuisine might be loosely described as a combination of Italian, Chinese, and Middle Eastern cooking. This attractive two-level restaurant has gold-leaf chandeliers, hanging brass pots, Asian rugs, and brass sconces. The dishes are memorable: delicate, deep-fried turnovers with stuffing of pumpkin or carrot; scallion-filled dumplings topped with yogurt and meat sauce; and a mélange of seasoned lamb garnished with pistachio nuts, almonds, orange strips, cardamom, and rose water. ✉ *1065 1st Ave., at 58th St.,* ☎ *212/644–9258;* ✉ *1437 2nd Ave., between 74th and 75th Sts.,* ☎ *212/734–3791. AE, DC, MC, V. No lunch Sat.–Mon.*

AMERICAN

$$$$
✕ **Rainbow Room.** This $25 million dinner-and-dancing room on the 65th floor remains a monument to glamour and fantasy. Tables clad in silver lamé rise in tiers around a revolving dance floor lit by an immense chandelier; aubergine walls frame panoramic views through floor-to-ceiling windows. Revamped retro dishes including lobster Thermidor and oysters Rockefeller contrast with specialties utilizing Hudson River valley produce (such as local cheeses, game, and New York State foie gras). ✉ *30 Rockefeller Plaza,* ☎ *212/632–5000 or 212/632–5100. Reservations essential. Jacket and tie. AE, DC, MC, V. Closed Mon. (Sun.–Mon. in summer).*

$$$$
★ ✕ **"21" Club.** If you're not known, the greeting at this four-story brownstone landmark, a former speakeasy, can be indifferent, even chilly. Once you're inside, though, service is seamless, and it's exciting to hobnob with celebrities and tycoons and sip a well-made cocktail in the lounge

before dinner. Here is one of the world's great wine cellars, with some 50,000 bottles. The Grill Room is *the* place to be, with its banquettes, red-checked tablecloths, and a ceiling hung with toys; it serves such standbys as the signature "21" burger. ⊠ *21 W. 52nd St.,* ☎ *212/582–7200. Reservations essential. Jacket and tie. AE, DC, MC, V. Closed Sun. No lunch Sat.*

\$\$–\$\$\$ ✕ **Judson Grill.** The airy space with a bar and balcony has
★ red velour banquettes, mirrored walls, lofty ceilings, engaging John Parks murals, and immense gold vases. The open kitchen produces sumptuous dishes like seared New York State foie gras and inventive seafood entrées, yet the more down-to-earth preparations—salads, sandwiches, and steaks—are equally well executed. ⊠ *152 W. 52nd St.,* ☎ *212/582–5252. AE, DC, MC, V. Closed Sun. No lunch Sat.*

CONTEMPORARY

\$\$\$–\$\$\$\$ ✕ **Four Seasons Grill and Pool Room.** The two unique din-
★ ing areas in the Mies van der Rohe–designed Seagram building feature architect Philip Johnson's timeless contemporary design. The Grill Room, bastion of the power lunch, also offers an affordable prix-fixe dinner. Starkly masculine, it has inviting leather banquettes, rosewood walls, a renowned floating sculpture, and one of the best bars in New York. The eclectic international menu changes often, and you'll appreciate the aristocratic wine list and smooth service. ⊠ *99 E. 52nd St.,* ☎ *212/754–9494. Reservations essential. Jacket required. AE, DC, MC, V. Closed Sun. No lunch Sat.*

FRENCH

\$\$\$\$ ✕ **La Côte Basque.** A landmark in French dining has found
★ a new home. Practically all the elements of the original restaurant have been imported, including the dark wooden cross beams, signature murals by Bernard Lamotte, and faux windows. Customers can partake of a reasonable (for such quality) fixed-price, three-course dinner, with very few surcharges. Begin with the trio of patés or one of the gossamer soufflés. If two select the signature roast duckling with honey, Grand Marnier, and black-cherry sauce, your waiter will deliver it whole for inspection and then carve it before you. ⊠ *60 W. 55th St., between 5th and 6th Aves.,* ☎

212/688–6525. Reservations essential. Jacket and tie. AE, DC, MC, V. No lunch Sun.

$$ ✕ **Cité.** This Art Deco Parisian-style brasserie with crystal chandeliers and imported grillwork (not to be confused with the more casual adjoining bistro) pours four wines with dinner free of charge. The wines change, but they're always top-drawer. An excellent three-course dinner is served from 8 PM to midnight. The food ranges from American steak house to Mediterranean, and since there's a real chef in the kitchen, you needn't stick to the excellent roast beef and sparkling shrimp or lobster cocktail. ✉ *120 W. 51st St.,* ☎ *212/956–7100. AE, DC, MC, V.*

JAPANESE

$$$$ ✕ **Otabe.** The sleek dining room has attractive wall prints and spacious seating. Among the appealing appetizers, try grilled eel on a bed of cucumber with a bouquet of fresh ginger or deep-fried tofu and eggplant. Adventurous souls will love the sparkling slices of raw tuna sashimi brushed with garlic-flavored soy sauce. Traditional Kyoto cuisine (a tasting menu of several small dishes) can be ordered, and in a room in back, you can experience superbly authentic *teppan* (barbecue-style grill) cooking. Here, you can spoil yourself with Kobe beef so tender knives are unnecessary. ✉ *68 E. 56th St.,* ☎ *212/223–7575. AE, DC, MC, V. Closed Sun. No lunch Sat.*

SEAFOOD

$$$–$$$$
★ ✕ **Sea Grill.** Famous restaurants with extraordinary views are often suspect when it comes to the food. But *this* famous restaurant, with a spectacular view of the Rockefeller Center ice rink in winter and captivating patio dining in summer, can stand tall. The kitchen creates some of Manhattan's best seafood dishes. Charred, moist sugarcane shrimp on skewers with buttery rice is a simple composition, prepared with complementing fresh herbs, spices, and a subtle sauce. We applaud the best lime pie this side of the Keys. ✉ *19 W. 49th St.,* ☎ *212/332–7610. Reservations essential. AE, DC, MC, V. Closed Sun. No lunch Sat.*

VIETNAMESE

$$–$$$ ✕ **Le Colonial.** The dining room here comes straight out of Somerset Maugham, with its rattan chairs, potted palms, ceiling fans, shutters, and period photographs. The food, although Westernized, is usually well prepared; start with the superb *bahn cuon*—steamed Vietnamese ravioli with chicken, shrimp, and mushrooms—and move on to crisp-seared whole snapper with spicy and sour sauce. The sorbets, ice creams, and fruit-based puddings are right on. ⊠ *149 E. 57th St.,* ☎ *212/752–0808. Reservations essential. AE, DC, MC, V.*

Theater District and Carnegie Hall

AMERICAN CASUAL

$ ✕ **Planet Hollywood.** This café is fun; its owners and shareholders include Bruce Willis, Demi Moore, Sylvester Stallone, Keith Barish, and Arnold Schwarzenegger. The walls are full of celebrity handprints outside and movie memorabilia inside; check out the gremlin. Who cares that the place rates a 10 on the decibel scale? The food is adequate; you'll be happiest if you stick with the southwestern-style nachos, the fajitas, and the playful pizzas. ⊠ *140 W. 57th St.,* ☎ *212/333–7827. AE, DC, MC, V.*

CONTEMPORARY

$$$ ✕ **Monkey Bar.** Cobalt-blue bread plates and glasses, ★ etched-glass panels of the Manhattan skyline, velvet banquettes with a colorful palm-tree design, and cute little monkeys hanging from the lighting fixtures all contribute to the lively atmosphere of this fashionable restaurant. You can bypass the mobbed bar scene by entering through the subdued Hotel Elysée. There's no monkey business going on with the food; perfectly roasted cod with silky mashed potatoes, carrots, and celery-root chips is recommended. ⊠ *60 E. 54th St.,* ☎ *212/838–2600. Reservations essential. Jacket required. AE, DC, MC, V. No lunch weekends.*

DELI

$ ✕ **Carnegie Deli.** Although not what it was, this no-nonsense spot is still one of midtown's two best delis, a species distinguished by crowds, noise, impatient service, and jumbo sandwiches. Ask the counterman to hand-slice your corned beef or pastrami; the extra juiciness and superior texture warrant the extra charge. To drink? Try cream soda or celery tonic. ⊠ *854 7th Ave., between 54th and 55th Sts.,* ☎ *212/757–2245. No credit cards.*

FRENCH

$$$–$$$$ ✕ **Petrossian.** This Art Deco caviar bar and restaurant is
★ like no other New York dining spot, with its fur-trimmed
banquettes, granite bar, profusion of marble, and contri-
butions of Erté and Lalique. You'll probably want to start
with gobs of fresh caviar: beluga, sevruga, or osetra, with
no competing garnishes. Petrossian offers an outstanding
prix-fixe dinner (one of the world's great bargains in lux-
ury dining) all evening; the supplement for 30 grams of
sevruga is relatively small. ⊠ *182 W. 58th St.,* ☎ *212/245–
2214. Reservations essential. AE, DC, MC, V.*

GREEK

$ ✕ **Uncle Nick's.** At this inexpensive taverna, you dine in a
★ long room, with a navy-blue pipe-lined tin ceiling, an exposed
kitchen, and a wood floor. Note the appetizing displays of
whole red snapper, porgy, and striped bass. Be sure to try as
many of the excellent appetizers as your tummy can handle,
including crispy fried smelts, tender grilled baby octopus, mar-
velous sweetbreads, and giant lima beans with tomatoes and
herbs. ⊠ *747 9th Ave., between 50th and 51st Sts.,* ☎ *212/
245–7992. MC, V.*

ITALIAN

$$$–$$$$ ✕ **Palio.** Named after the 800-year-old Italian horse race
★ that celebrates the Assumption of the Virgin, this excep-
tional restaurant has an impressive 13-ft mural by Sandro
Chia. Your name is discretely requested as you're ushered
to an elevator and the second-floor dining room with light
oak paneling and luxuriously spaced tables set with Frette
linen and Riedel crystal. Here you'll experience authentic
Italian cuisine, from a regional six-course menu from Siena
to one based on aged balsamic vinegar. ⊠ *151 W. 51st St.,*
☎ *212/245–4850. Reservations essential. Jacket and tie.
AE, DC, MC, V. Closed Sun. No lunch Sat.*

$$–$$$ ✕ **Trattoria Dell'Arte.** This popular trattoria near Carnegie
★ Hall still displays the controversial oversize renderings of
body parts, alongside portraits of Italian artists, in its three
dining rooms. But you'll probably be more interested in the

mouthwatering antipasti on the bar and the tasty pasta, pizza, hot focaccia sandwiches, and grilled double veal chop, served with a mountain of shoestring potatoes. The cannoli is wonderful. ⊠ *900 7th Ave., between 56th and 57th Sts.,* ☎ *212/245–9800. Reservations essential. AE, DC, MC, V.*

LATIN

$ ✕ **Pomaire.** Named after a small village renowned for its pottery (in which many of the dishes are served), this uncommon restaurant with exposed brick, handmade rugs, a faux skylight, and attractive paintings sometimes offers live music. The menu lists several intriguing dinner options, such as *pastel de choclo,* a casserole of beef, olives, chicken, onions, and egg that is covered with a corn puree, dusted with sugar, and baked in a clay pot. Leave room for *torta de mil hojas*—leaves of pastry layered with caramel. ⊠ *371 W. 46th St., off 9th Ave.,* ☎ *212/956–3056. AE, DC, MC, V. No lunch.*

STEAK

$$$–$$$$ ✕ **Ben Benson's.** Witness such contemporary steak-house
★   fare as cold lobster cocktail and Maryland crab cakes, steaks, chops, and the fabulous prime rib, as well as such excellent daily specials as Friday's crusted fish hash. Don't miss the horseradish mashed potatoes or the excellent home fries. This convivial spot has a masculine interior—brass plaques inscribed with names of celebrities and framed pictures of animals and game birds. ⊠ *123 W. 52nd St.,* ☎ *212/581–8888. Reservations essential. AE, DC, MC, V. No lunch weekends.*

Upper East Side

CHINESE

$–$$ ✕ **Evergreen Cafe.** Come here for the Chinatown-style dumplings (try asparagus or seafood fillings) and the full range of noodle and rice dishes, such as Singapore-style curry-flavored noodles or diced chicken in salted fish-flavor fried rice. This attractive restaurant has blond wood tables, ceiling fans, and an illuminated emerald sculpture; the back dining room tends to be more quiet. ⊠ *1288 1st Ave., at 69th St.,* ☎ *212/744–3266. AE, DC, MC, V.*

CONTEMPORARY

$$$ ✕ **Jo Jo.** New York's most fashionable bistro has an up-
★ stairs dining area with burgundy banquettes, a black-and-
white tile floor, and the obligatory etched-glass and gilt-edge
mirrors. Celebrity-chef Jean-Georges Vongerichten follows
a culinary approach that is personal (French with Asian ac-
cents), healthy (infused oils, juices, and reduction rather than
heavy sauces), and classic (hardy bistro dishes freely up-
dated). Goat-cheese-and-potato terrine is typical of Von-
gerichten's culinary range, as are the signature shrimp in
spiced-carrot juice and Thai lime leaves, and the simple
chicken roasted with ginger, green olives, and ginger juice,
accompanied by chickpea-tahini fritters. ✉ *160 E. 64th St.,*
☎ *212/223–5656. Reservations essential. AE, MC, V.
Closed Sun. No lunch Sat.*

$$$ ✕ **Sign of the Dove.** Skylights, stunning floral arrange-
★ ments, brick arches, and piano music lend a distinctive
character to each of the dining rooms here, some of the pret-
tiest in town. Don't miss the singular preparations of tuna
(at times in aromatic broth with Asian vegetables), the
low-cholesterol venison dish, or the omnipresent warm
chocolate soufflé cake with house-made vanilla ice cream.
Prix-fixe menus put this place squarely among the city's best
famous-restaurant values. ✉ *1110 3rd Ave., at 65th St.,*
☎ *212/861–8080. Reservations essential. AE, DC, MC,
V. No lunch Mon.*

FRENCH

$$$$ ✕ **Daniel.** At Daniel Boulud's $1.9 million restaurant, lav-
★ ish flower arrangements, antique mirrors, and wall-to-wall
celebrities adorn the main dining room, with its exquisite
table settings by Limoges, gold-tinted walls, and red-checked
banquettes. The cuisine (at once contemporary and classic) is among the best in New York. Note the uncommon
tuna tartare, with a touch of curry, and the signature black
sea bass, wrapped in a crispy potato shell. Spoil yourself
with the all-chocolate or all-fruit dessert menu. ✉ *20 E.
76th St.,* ☎ *212/288–0033. Reservations essential. Jacket
required. AE, D, DC, MC, V. Closed Sun. No lunch Mon.*

$$–$$$ ✕ **L'Absinthe.** The wonderful Art Nouveau bistro decor fea-
★ tures etched glass, huge gilt-framed mirrors, tile floors,
and a few sidewalk tables. Highlights on the menu include

a fine foie gras terrine, slow-braised beef with carrots, poached free-range chicken in truffle broth, and a thin, crisp apple tart or warm chocolate cake. ⊠ *227 E. 67th St.,* ☎ *212/794–4950. Reservations essential. AE, MC, V.*

MIDDLE EASTERN

$ ✕ **Afghan Kebab House #2.** At this cavelike Afghan restaurant, scenic posters, copper platters, and Afghan rugs cover the walls. Newcomers to this cuisine should enjoy the *aushak,* or boiled dumplings, filled with scallions, herbs, and spices and topped with yogurt; the spiced half-chicken, marinated in fresh grated spices and hot peppers; and the vegetable combination plate. ⊠ *1345 2nd Ave., between 70th and 71st Sts.,* ☎ *212/517–2776. AE, DC, MC, V. BYOB.*

$ ✕ **Persepolis.** Manhattan's only authentic Persian restaurant has been artfully decorated with smoked-glass mirrors, huge globe light fixtures, and carpeted banquettes. Make an effort to order as many appetizers as you can handle, and don't omit baba ghanoush, *torshi* (pickled carrots, eggplant, celery, garlic, and parsley), and the olive salad. The Persepolis kebab (filet mignon, chopped steak, and chicken) on skewers exemplifies this delicate and choice cuisine. ⊠ *1423 2nd Ave., between 74th and 75th Sts.,* ☎ *212/ 535–1100. AE, DC, MC, V.*

PIZZA

$ ✕ **Sofia Fabulous Pizza.** Mediterranean-colored friezes
★ grace this trendy café with wine racks, a vaulted ceiling, and wall sconces made of Japanese paper. In the breathtaking thin-crust pizza, prepared with filtered water to resemble the dough of Naples, Sofia uses mozzarella made daily with fresh milk. For a singular treat, try the mashed potatoes slathered with homemade tomato sauce and Parmesan cheese and then baked in the oven. ⊠ *1022 Madison Ave., near 79th St.,* ☎ *212/734–2676. AE, DC, MC, V.*

STEAK

$$$–$$$$ ✕ **Manhattan Café.** You enter this steak house through a
★ bronze doorway that belonged to the old Biltmore hotel. Cut flowers, Art Deco chandeliers, Persian carpets, and deep hunter-green upholstery are a far cry from the rush-and-crush

Uptown Manhattan Dining

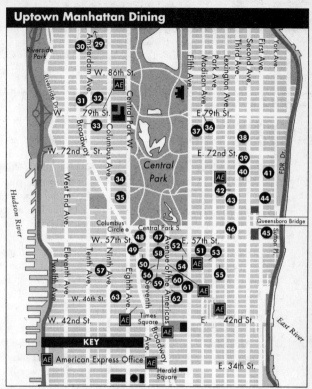

Afghan Kebab House #2, **39**
Ben Benson's, **56**
Café des Artistes, **34**
Carmine's, **30**
Carnegie Deli, **50**
Cité, **60**
Daniel, **37**
Evergreen Cafe, **41**

Four Seasons Grill and Pool Room, **55**
Gabriela's, **29**
Jo Jo, **43**
Judson Grill, **58**
L'Absinthe, **40**
La Côte Basque, **52**
Le Colonial, **46**
Mad Fish, **33**
Manhattan Café, **44**

Monkey Bar, **53**
Otabe, **51**
Palio, **59**
Pamir, **45**
Persepolis, **38**
Petrossian, **48**
Picholine, **35**
Planet Hollywood, **47**
Pomaire, **63**
Rainbow Room, **61**

Savann, **32**
Sea Grill, **62**
Sign of the Dove, **42**
Sofia Fabulous Pizza, **36**
Stingray, **31**
Trattoria Dell'Arte, **49**
"21" Club, **54**
Uncle Nick's, **57**

atmosphere of most of its competitors. Steaks are among the best in town. And don't overlook the well-prepared seafood dishes, Lyonnaise potatoes, and some savory Italian specialties. ⊠ *1161 1st Ave., between 63rd and 64th Sts.,* ☎ *212/888–6556. AE, DC, MC, V. No lunch Sat.*

Lincoln Center

CONTINENTAL

$$$–$$$$ ✕ **Café des Artistes.** Writer–restaurant consultant George
★   Lang's masterpiece, this most European of cafés provides a snug and beautiful ambience with its polished oak woodwork and rosy Howard Chandler Christy murals of nymphs at play. The cuisine is as refined as the setting. Four-way salmon, with tidbits of the fish that are smoked, poached, dill-marinated, or raw, is a perfect introduction, and it would be hard to find a better pot-au-feu. For dessert, request the mocha *dacquoise* (layers of hazelnut meringue, sandwiched together with French buttercream). Customers adore the especially festive brunch. ⊠ *1 W. 67th St.,* ☎ *212/877–3500. Reservations essential. Jacket required. AE, DC, MC, V.*

MEDITERRANEAN

$$$–$$$$ ✕ **Picholine.** Named for a small green Mediterranean olive,
★   this mellow restaurant is patterned on a Provençal farmhouse, with soft colors, wood floors, and dried flowers. Top dishes include the signature grilled octopus with fennel, potato, and lemon-pepper dressing; Moroccan-spiced loin of lamb with vegetable couscous and mint-yogurt sauce; and tournedos of salmon with horseradish crust, cucumbers, and salmon caviar. The cheese selection of some 30 varieties, in prime condition and served at room temperature, is indicative of a devotion to quality. ⊠ *35 W. 64th St., off Broadway,* ☎ *212/724–8585. Reservations essential. AE, DC, MC, V. Closed Sun. No lunch Mon.*

Upper West Side

FRENCH

$–$$ ✕ **Savann.** The dining area has exposed brick, brass ceiling
★   ing fans, and track lighting. Among the superb entrées are cornmeal-crusted oysters on creamy celery-root puree and

pan-roasted medallions of salmon with spaghetti squash in a roasted tomato vinaigrette. Apple tarte Tatin with cinnamon ice cream makes a wonderful finale. (Savann Est is found at 181 East 78th Street, ☏ 212/396–9300.) ⊠ *414 Amsterdam Ave., at 80th St., ☏ 212/580–0202. AE, MC, V. No lunch.*

ITALIAN

$–$$ ✕ **Carmine's.** Dark woodwork and old-fashioned black-and-
★ white tiles make this hot spot look like an old-timer. It isn't. Still, savvy West Siders are only too glad to line up for its home-style cooking, served family style. Kick off a meal with fried calamari or stuffed artichoke; then move on to the pastas or lobster *fra diabolo* (in a spicy tomato sauce). ⊠ *2450 Broadway, between 90th and 91st Sts., ☏ 212/362–2200; ⊠ 200 W. 44th St., between Broadway and 8th Ave., ☏ 212/221–3800. Reservations only for 6 or more. AE. No lunch.*

MEXICAN

$ ✕ **Gabriela's.** This modest cantina with ceramic parrots
★ hanging from the ceiling and a desert wall mural will reward lovers of authentic Mexican cuisine. The menu has wonderful tacos, stuffed with beef tongue and *chicharron* (deep-fried pork skins) in a memorable bath of tomatillo and serrano sauce. The house specialty is a whole rotisserie chicken, Yucatán style, with rice, beans, and plantains. ⊠ *685 Amsterdam Ave., at 93rd St., ☏ 212/961–0574. AE, DC, MC, V.*

SEAFOOD

$$ ✕ **Mad Fish.** This seafood spot has a skylit shingled roof and amusing murals depicting cocktail parties with fish as the guests. At the long mahogany bar, you can sample boiled periwinkles, steamed lobster, seasonal oysters, and more. The kitchen produces stylish food, such as barbecued bluefish and fish-and-chips—cured fresh cod, gently coated with tempura and quickly deep-fried. Be sure to sample the warm flourless chocolate cake. ⊠ *2182 Broadway, between 77th and 78th Sts., ☏ 212/787–0202. AE, DC, MC, V. No lunch.*

$–$$ ✕ **Stingray.** This trendy restaurant has mottled gold walls, a copper-color tin ceiling, and comfortably upholstered redwood chairs. The most commanding area is the lounge, with its cane chairs, colorful tile mosaics, and small cocktail tables. The eclectic food runs the gamut from oysters on the half shell with caper mignonette and green horseradish sour cream to grilled lobsters with roasted corn and tomato salsa. ⊠ *428 Amsterdam Ave., between 80th and 81st Sts.,* ☏ *212/501–7515. AE, DC, MC, V.*

4 Lodging

By Amy
McConnell

IF ANY SINGLE ELEMENT OF YOUR TRIP to New York City will cost you dearly, it will be your hotel room. Unlike many European cities, New York offers few low-priced lodgings. Real estate is at a premium here, and labor costs are high, so hoteliers start out with a lot of expenses to cover. And considering the healthy occupancy rate, market forces are not likely to drive current prices down. Fleabags and flophouses aside, there's precious little here for less than $100 a night. The city doesn't charge the highest hotel tax in the country, but you should not fail to figure the 13¼% combined taxes plus $2 per room, per night (city occupancy charge) into your calculations. We have scoured the city for good-value hotels and budget properties, but even our $ category includes hotels that run as high as $135 for one night's stay in a double.

Our price categories are based on the "rack rate," or the standard room cost that hotels print in their brochures and quote over the phone. You almost never need to pay this much. If you book directly with the hotel, ask about corporate rates, seasonal special offers, or weekend deals. The last typically include such extras as complimentary meals, drinks, or tickets to events. Ask your travel agent for brochures, and look for advertisements in travel magazines or the Sunday travel sections of major newspapers such as the *New York Times,* the *Washington Post,* or the *Los Angeles Times.* If you should be unfortunate enough to arrive in New York City without a hotel reservation, you can also try the most direct method of lowering the room rate: asking. In periods of low occupancy, hotels—especially at the expensive end of the market—will often reduce the price on rooms that would otherwise remain empty.

In general, Manhattan hotels don't measure up to those in other U.S. cities in terms of room size, parking, or outside landscaping. But, since this is a sophisticated city, they usually compensate with fastidious service, sprucely maintained properties, and restaurants that hold their own in a city of knowledgeable diners.

Note: Even the most exclusive hotels have security gaps. Be discreet with valuables everywhere, and stay alert in public areas.

CATEGORY	COST*
$$$$	over $260
$$$	$190–$260
$$	$135–$190
$	under $135

All prices are for a standard double room, excluding 13¼% city and state taxes.

Reservations

New York is constantly full of vacationers, conventioneers, and business travelers, all requiring hotel space. Try to book your room as far in advance as possible, using a major credit card to guarantee the reservation; you might even want to work through a travel agent. Because this is a tight market, overbooking can be a problem, and "lost" reservations are not unheard of. When signing in, take a pleasant but firm attitude; if there is a mix-up, chances are the outcome will be an upgrade or a free night.

Services

Unless otherwise noted in the individual descriptions, all the hotels listed have the following features and services: private baths, central heating, air-conditioning, private telephones, no-smoking rooms or floors, on-premises dining, room service (though not necessarily 24-hour or short-notice), TV (including cable and pay-per-view films), and a routine concierge staff. Almost all hotels now have dataports and phones with voice mail. Hotels in the higher price categories generally offer baby-sitting (arranged through the concierge) and valet service. Most large hotels have video or high-speed checkout capability. Pools are a rarity, but most properties have fitness centers; we note only those that are on the premises, but other hotels usually have arrangements for guests at nearby facilities, for which a fee is sometimes charged.

Those bringing a car to Manhattan should note the lack of hotel parking. Many properties in all price ranges *do* have parking facilities, but they are often at independent garages that charge as much as $20 or more per day. A few hotels offer free parking; they are noted in the following reviews.

Midtown East

$$$$ ⊞ **Four Seasons.** Architect I. M. Pei—responsible for the
★   Louvre Pyramid, among other modernist icons—designed
           this limestone-clad stepped spire amid the prime shops of
           57th Street. Everything here comes in epic proportions—
           from the prices (it's New York's most expensive hotel); to
           the guest rooms, which average 600 square ft; to the aptly
           named, sky-high Grand Foyer, with its French limestone pil-
           lars, marble, onyx, and acre upon acre of blond wood. The
           soundproof guest rooms offer the ultimate in luxury, with
           enormous English sycamore walk-in closets, 10-ft-high
           ceilings, and spacious bathrooms with tubs that fill in 60
           seconds. ⊠ *57 E. 57th St., 10022,* ☎ *212/758–5700 or
           800/332–3442,* ⨳ *212/758–5711. 370 rooms. Restaurant,
           bar, in-room safes, minibars, spa, business services, meet-
           ing rooms. AE, DC, MC, V.*

$$$$ ⊞ **New York Palace.** A multimillion-dollar renovation
           completed in spring 1997 transformed this hotel into one
           of New York's finest. Long known for its landmark 1882
           Villard House, which contains many of the hotel's public
           rooms, the Palace now offers one of the city's most elabo-
           rate hotel health clubs and a new lobby restaurant; in ad-
           dition, the celebrated Le Cirque restaurant is now in the
           Villard House. The newly redecorated guest rooms are large
           by Manhattan standards; those on the west side afford
           views of St. Patrick's Cathedral and Rockefeller Center. All
           are equipped with fax machines. ⊠ *455 Madison Ave.,
           10022,* ☎ *212/888–7000 or 800/697–2522,* ⨳ *212/303–
           6000. 900 rooms. 2 restaurants, 2 bars, breakfast room, in-
           room safes, minibars, spa, business services, meeting rooms.
           AE, D, DC, MC, V.*

$$$–$$$$ ⊞ **Waldorf-Astoria.** This landmark Art Deco masterpiece
           serves as a hub of city life; the lobby, with its original mu-
           rals and mosaics and elaborate plaster ornamentation, is a
           meeting place for the rich and powerful. Guest rooms, each
           individually decorated but all traditional and elegant, start
           at the low end of the $$$ category. Astoria-level rooms
           have the added advantages of great views, fax machines, and
           access to the Astoria lounge, where a lovely afternoon tea
           is served free. The Tower section, well known to heads of
           state and discerning business travelers, is the most exclusive
           and grand section of the hotel. ⊠ *301 Park Ave., 10022,*

The Algonquin, **22**

Beekman
Tower, **20**

Broadway Bed &
Breakfast, **14**

The Carlyle, **6**

Doral Park
Avenue, **26**

Dumont
Plaza, **28**

Eastgate
Tower, **25**

Essex House, **8**

The Excelsior, **1**

The
Fitzpatrick, **15**

Four Seasons, **12**

The Franklin, **37**

The Gershwin, **32**

Gramercy
Park Hotel, **33**

Herald Square
Hotel, **31**

Hotel Beacon, **3**

Hotel Edison, **13**

Hotel Wales, **36**

Jolly Madison
Towers, **27**

Larchmont
Hotel, **29**

The Mansfield, **23**

The Mark, **4**

Mayflower, **7**

The Milburn, **2**

New York
Palace, **18**

The
Paramount, **21**

Park Savoy, **11**

Pickwick Arms
Hotel, **17**

The Plaza, **10**

Portland Square
Hotel, **16**

Ritz-Carlton, **9**

The Royalton, **24**

SoHo Grand, **34**

Southgate
Tower, **30**

Surrey Hotel, **5**

Waldorf-
Astoria, **19**

Washington
Square Hotel, **35**

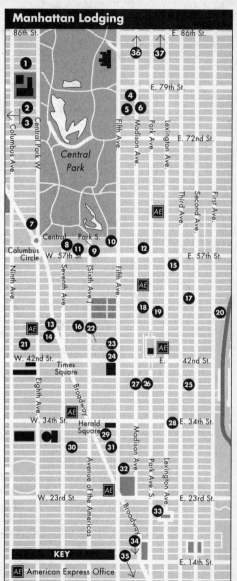

Manhattan Lodging

KEY

AE American Express Office

☎ 212/355–3000 or 800/925–3673, ℻ 212/872–7272. *1,380 rooms. 4 restaurants, minibars, health club, business services, meeting rooms. AE, D, DC, MC, V.*

$$$ 🏨 **The Fitzpatrick.** This cozy hotel just south of Bloom-
★ ingdale's, the first American venture for an established Irish company, is a winner in terms of value and charm. More than half of the units are true suites that are priced well below the market average, even on weekdays. All have emerald green carpets, traditional furnishings, and modern, well-equipped bathrooms. The mostly Irish staff is exceptionally friendly and cheerful, which might explain why Gregory Peck, Liam Neeson, various Kennedys, Sinead O'Connor, and the Chieftains have all been guests. ✉ *687 Lexington Ave., 10022,* ☎ *212/355–0100 or 800/367– 7701,* ℻ *212/355–1371. 92 rooms. Restaurant, bar, meeting room. AE, D, DC, MC, V.*

$ 🏨 **Pickwick Arms Hotel.** This convenient East Side establishment charges $99 a night for standard doubles and has older singles with shared baths for as little as $50. The marble-clad lobby is often bustling, since this place is routinely booked solid by bargain hunters. Privations you endure to save a buck start and end with the Lilliputian size of some rooms, all of which have cheap-looking furnishings. However, the place is well run and safe, and some rooms look over the Manhattan skyline. ✉ *230 E. 51st St., 10022,* ☎ *212/355–0300 or 800/742–5945,* ℻ *212/755–5029. 370 rooms. Café. AE, DC, MC, V.*

Midtown West

$$$ 🏨 **The Algonquin.** This beloved landmark hotel, where the Round Table group of writers and wits once met for lunch, still shelters celebrities, particularly literary types visiting nearby publishing houses or the *New Yorker* magazine offices. The heartbeat of the hotel is the lobby, with its grandfather clock, overstuffed chairs, and house cat, Matilda. Rooms have homey, Victorian-style fixtures and furnishings; specialty suites are dedicated to Dorothy Parker, James Thurber, and *Vanity Fair.* Continental breakfast is complimentary. ✉ *59 W. 44th St., 10036,* ☎ *212/840–6800 or 800/548–0345,* ℻ *212/944–1618. 165 rooms. 2 restaurants, bar, in-room safes, cabaret, library, business services,* *meeting rooms, free parking (weekends only). AE, D, DC, MC, V.*

$$$ ▣ **The Mansfield.** Built in 1904 as lodging for well-heeled bachelors, this small hotel is Victorian and clublike. Turn-of-the-century details abound here: from the column-supported coffered ceiling, warm ivory walls, and yellow limestone floor in the lobby to the guest rooms' black marble bathrooms, ebony-stained floors and doors, dark-wood venetian blinds, and sleigh beds. There are movies in the audiovisual lounge and nightly piano and harp recitals in the intimate concert salon, where complimentary breakfast and after-theater dessert are served. ⊠ *12 W. 44th St., 10036,* ☎ *212/944–6050 or 800/255–5167,* FAX *212/764–4477. 123 rooms. In-room VCRs, cinema, concert hall, library, free parking. AE, MC, V.*

$$$ ▣ **The Paramount.** The work of the team responsible for
★   the Royalton (☞ *below*), the fashionable Paramount caters to the forever young and arty. In the Philippe Starck lobby, a sheer platinum wall and a glamorous sweep of staircase lead to a mezzanine gallery of squashy seating, tiny nightclub-style table lamps, and a restaurant—the perfect place to spy on the glitterati below. Rooms are minute, but they have framed headboards, several of them bearing the print of Vermeer's *The Lacemaker,* and conical steel sinks in the bathrooms—all bearing the Starck stamp. ⊠ *235 W. 46th St., 10036,* ☎ *212/764–5500 or 800/225–7474,* FAX *212/575–4892. 610 rooms. 2 restaurants, bar, café, in-room VCRs, exercise room, nursery, business services. AE, D, DC, MC, V.*

$$$ ▣ **The Royalton.** Ian Schrager and the late Steve Rubell's second Manhattan hotel is a second home to the world's media, music, and fashion-biz folk. The centerpiece of each Philippe Starck–designed guest room is a low-lying, custom-made bed with built-in pin lights; there are also geometrically challenged but comfy blue velvet chairs, and window banquettes. The staff does a good job catering to people who feel it's their lot in life to be waited on. The restaurant, 44, is predictably booked solid by New York–style gurus. ⊠ *44 W. 44th St., 10036,* ☎ *212/869–4400 or 800/635–9013,* FAX *212/575–0012. 168 rooms. Restaurant, bar, minibars, exercise room, meeting rooms. AE, DC, MC, V.*

$ **Broadway Bed & Breakfast.** In the heart of the theater district, this reasonably priced B&B is friendly and comfortable. Continental breakfast is served in the Victorian-style lobby, where brick walls, stocked bookshelves, and framed photos of old New York encourage lingering. The building, which dates from 1918, was completely renovated in 1995, and everything from the freshly painted and carpeted rooms to the gleaming dark-wood stair banisters is meticulously maintained. ⊠ *264 W. 46th St., 10036,* ☎ *212/997–9200 or 800/826–6300,* 𝐅𝐀𝐗 *212/768–2807. 40 rooms. Breakfast room. AE, D, DC, MC, V.*

$ **Herald Square Hotel.** Sculpted cherubs on its facade and vintage magazine covers adorning the hallways inside lend character to this historic hotel, which is housed in the former *Life* magazine building. Rooms are basic and clean, with deep-green carpets and floral-print bedspreads; all have TVs, phones with voice mail, and in-room safes. There's no concierge and no room service, but what does it matter when rooms cost as little as $89? ⊠ *19 W. 31st St., 10001,* ☎ *212/279–4017 or 800/727–1888,* 𝐅𝐀𝐗 *212/ 643–9208. 127 rooms. In-room safes. AE, D, MC, V.*

$ **Hotel Edison.** This offbeat old hotel is a popular budget stop for domestic and international tour groups. The loan-shark murder scene in *The Godfather* was shot in what is now Sophia's restaurant, and the pink-plaster coffee shop is a hot place to eavesdrop on show-business gossip. Guest rooms are clean and fresh; bathrooms are miniscule. There's no room service, but this part of the theater district has so many restaurants and delis that it doesn't matter much. ⊠ *228 W. 47th St., 10036,* ☎ *212/840–5000 or 800/637–7070,* 𝐅𝐀𝐗 *212/596–6850. 1,000 rooms. Restaurant, bar, coffee shop, beauty salon, airport shuttle. AE, D, DC, MC, V.*

$ **Park Savoy.** Rooms here cost as little as $57 (rates go up to $126), and you're in close proximity to Central Park, Carnegie Hall, and the caviar at Petrossian. This more than makes up for the lack of room service, direct-dial phone, and cable TV channels. Room decor is eclectic (William Morris–pattern drapes, wine-color carpet, and rock-hard beds). The staff (okay, the guy at the desk) knows all the guests, and there's a lot of repeat business. ⊠ *158 W. 58th St., 10019,* ☎ *212/245–5755,* 𝐅𝐀𝐗 *212/765–0668. 96 rooms. AE, MC, V.*

$ ▣ **Portland Square Hotel.** You can't beat this theater district old-timer for value, with its clean, simple rooms, exercise facility (albeit tiny), coin laundry, and business services. James Cagney lived in the building, and—as the story goes—a few of his Radio City Rockette acquaintances lived upstairs. Rooms have green carpets and floral-print bedspreads; those on the east wing have oversize bathrooms. ✉ *132 W. 47th St., 10036,* ☎ *212/382–0600 or 800/388–8988,* FAX *212/382–0684. 142 rooms. In-room safes, exercise room, coin laundry. AE, MC, V.*

Central Park South/59th Street

$$$$ ▣ **Essex House.** The owners, Japan's Nikko Hotels, have
★ done wonders for this stately Central Park South property. The public areas are Art Deco masterpieces fit for Fred and Ginger. The talented Christian Delouvrier oversees the cuisine, both in the informal Café Botanica (which faces Central Park and resembles a lush prewar English greenhouse) and in the acclaimed Les Célébrités, where art painted by luminaries covers the walls. Guest rooms resemble those in a splendid English country home, elegant and inviting. The staff is discreet, efficient, and friendly. ✉ *160 Central Park S, between 6th and 7th Aves., 10019,* ☎ *212/247–0300,* FAX *212/315–1839. 597 rooms. 2 restaurants, bar, in-room safes, minibars, in-room VCRs, spa, business services, meeting rooms. AE, D, DC, MC, V.*

$$$$ ▣ **The Plaza.** With its unsurpassed location opposite Central Park and F.A.O. Schwarz, the Plaza is probably the most high-profile of all New York hotels. Donald Trump bought it (in 1988), the fictional Eloise ran riot in it, and film upon film has featured it. Its legendary reputation is well deserved: Even the smallest guest rooms have crystal chandeliers and 14-ft-high ceilings. A stroll by the fin-de-siècle Palm Court or a view of the park and 5th Avenue from a table in the Edwardian Room will give you a sense of what makes the city tick. ✉ *5th Ave. at 59th St., 10019,* ☎ *212/759–3000 or 800/759–3000,* FAX *212/546–5324. 805 rooms. 3 restaurants, 2 bars, café, minibars, exercise room, business services, meeting rooms. AE, D, DC, MC, V.*

$$$$ ▣ **Ritz-Carlton.** Everything about this hotel is first-class, from
★ the prestigious Central Park South address to the very pol-

ished service to the fine art that covers virtually every wall. Guest rooms are graced with rich brocades, polished woods, and marble bathrooms; some have breathtaking Central Park views. The restaurant, Fantino, serves award-winning cuisine on china designed by Gianni Versace. ⊠ *112 Central Park S, 10019,* ☎ *212/757–1900 or 800/241–3333,* FAX *212/ 757–9620. 214 rooms. Restaurant, bar, health club, business services, meeting rooms. AE, D, DC, MC, V.*

Upper East Side

$$$$ ▦ **The Carlyle.** European tradition and Manhattan swank
★ shake hands at New York's least hysterical grand hotel. Everything about this Madison Avenue landmark suggests refinement, from the Mark Hampton–designed rooms, with their fine antique furniture and artfully framed Audubons and botanicals, to the first-rate service, which combines old-school elegance with genuine friendliness. Many guests head straight to the beloved Bemelmans Bar, named after Ludwig Bemelmans, illustrator of the beloved children's book character Madeline and the "twelve little girls in two straight lines"; he created the murals here. Others come just to hear Barbara Cook or Bobby Short perform at the clubby Café Carlyle. ⊠ *35 E. 76th St., 10021,* ☎ *212/744–1600 or 800/227–5737,* FAX *212/717–4682. 190 rooms. Restaurant, bar, café, kitchenettes, minibars, spa, meeting rooms. AE, DC, MC, V.*

$$$$ ▦ **The Mark.** You'll find this friendly baby grand hotel a block
★ north of the Carlyle and steps from Central Park. The feeling of calm that pervades the Biedermeier-furnished marble lobby follows you into the deep-green and burgundy bar, where even lone women travelers feel comfortable. The serenity continues at Mark's Restaurant, where afternoon tea is an institution. Bedrooms are elegant and serene, with cream-colored walls, museum-quality prints, plump armchairs, a potted palm or two, and Belgian bed linens. ⊠ *25 E. 77th St., 10021,* ☎ *212/744–4300 or 800/843–6275,* FAX *212/ 744–2749. 180 rooms. Restaurant, minibars, in-room VCRs, health club, meeting rooms. AE, D, DC, MC, V.*

$$–$$$ ▦ **Hotel Wales.** In the tony neighborhood of Carnegie Hill, this modestly priced hotel is a pleasant surprise. It occupies a landmark building, and every effort has been made to retain the turn-of-the-century mood—from the fin-de-siè-cle-style lobby to the "Pied Piper" parlor, where vintage children's illustrations cover the walls. Bathrooms are miniscule, and guest rooms are slightly the worse for wear, but fireplaces and fine oak woodwork make up for these faults. A generous European-style breakfast and nightly dessert buffet are served in the parlor. ⊠ *1295 Madison Ave., 10128,* ☎ *212/876–6000 or 800/528–5252,* FAX *212/860–7000. 86 rooms. Breakfast room, in-room VCRs. AE, MC, V.*

$$ 🖼 **The Franklin.** It's like sleeping in an art installation. This formerly seedy, low-rent hostel was transformed into its current incarnation as a ravishing, funky, uptown version of the Paramount. The lobby feels like a private club, with black granite, brushed steel, and cherry-wood decor. Rooms can be very, very small (some measuring 100 square ft), but they have pleasant grape-colored carpeting, custom-built steel furniture, gauzy white canopies over the beds, and cedar closets. ⊠ *164 E. 87th St., 10128,* ☎ *212/369–1000 or 800/428–5252,* FAX *212/369–8000. 47 rooms. Breakfast room, in-room VCRs, library, free parking. AE, MC, V.*

Upper West Side

$$ 🖼 **Mayflower.** After you step under this hotel's green
★ awning into the long, low, wood-paneled lobby, with its gilt-framed oils of tall ships and flowers, you can take an apple from the basket on the registration desk and feel truly welcomed to New York. Such is the charm of this friendly hotel on Central Park. Rooms are large, with thick carpeting, fruit-and-flower-print drapes, dark-wood Colonial-style furniture, and walk-in closets; most include walk-in pantries with a fridge and sink. Spend an extra $20 for a spectacular park view. ⊠ *15 Central Park W, 10023,* ☎ *212/265–0060 or 800/223–4164,* FAX *212/265–2026. 365 rooms. Restaurant, bar, refrigerators, exercise room, meeting rooms. AE, DC, MC, V.*

$ 🖼 **The Excelsior.** The Excelsior is like one of those faded atmospheric hotels you often find on Parisian backstreets, but it's in a prime New York location: directly across from the American Museum of Natural History. Bedrooms are painted icy blue—a color that's made colder still by the harsh light of electricity-saving bulbs. Still, you can't beat the great staff, great neighborhood, and great rates. ⊠ *45 W. 81st St., 10024,* ☎ *212/362–9200 or 800/368–4575,* ℻ *212/721–2994. 160 rooms. Coffee shop. AE, MC, V.*

$ 🖭 **Hotel Beacon.** Three blocks from both Central Park
★   and Lincoln Center, this lodging offers many more amenities than you'd expect in this price category. The large rooms and the suites, which have kitchenettes with coffeemakers, full-size refrigerators, and stoves, cost only $40 more than standard rooms. The closets are huge, the dark-wood furniture is elegant, and the bathrooms come complete with Hollywood dressing room–style mirrors. There is no restaurant or bar, but with so much in the neighborhood, this isn't a problem. ⊠ *2130 Broadway, at 75th St., 10023,* ☎ *212/787–1100 or 800/572–4969,* ℻ *212/724–0839. 198 rooms. Refrigerators, meeting room. AE, D, DC, MC, V.*

$ 🖭 **The Milburn.** Convenient to Lincoln Center, Central Park, and Zabar's, this bohemian little hotel has a lobby that looks like a small Bavarian castle, with salmon-pink walls, black-and-white marble floor, heraldic doodads, and abundant gilt. The homey, spacious rooms are a chaotic but cozy assemblage of, say, burgundy carpet and blue drapes, a glass-top brass table, and framed posters on pink floral walls. All have kitchenettes equipped with, among other things, a microwave and coffeemaker. ⊠ *242 W. 76th St., 10023,* ☎ *212/362–1006 or 800/833–9622,* ℻ *212/721–5476. 102 rooms. Kitchenettes. AE, DC, MC, V.*

Murray Hill and Gramercy Park

$$$ 🖭 **Doral Park Avenue.** This stately little hotel on Park Avenue is stylish in an amusing way. The look is neoclassical
★   meets Miami—from the lobby rotunda, with its giant painting of an ancient Greek city offset by palm trees and art deco details, to the renovated guest rooms, some of which combine neoclassical headboards with faux-leopard-skin windowseat coverings. Newer rooms have a French country–style decor. The swank Odyssey Lounge has bright red walls topped with a neoclassical frieze as well as big windows facing Park Avenue. ⊠ *70 Park Ave., at 38th St., 10016,* ☎ *212/687–7050 or 800/223–6725,* ℻ *212/973–2497. 188 rooms. Restaurant, breakfast room, health club, meeting rooms. AE, D, DC, MC, V.*

$$–$$$ ⊞ **Manhattan East Suite Hotels.** These nine full-service hotels are residential with low rates for long stays. They vary in character and price, though most reach the upper end of the $$$ category in busy seasons. Best bets are **Beekman Tower** (⊠ 3 Mitchell Pl.), near the United Nations; **Dumont Plaza** (⊠ 150 E. 34th St.); **Surrey Hotel** (⊠ 20 E. 76th St.), which is close to Madison Avenue and borders on truly elegant; **Southgate Tower** (⊠ 371 7th Ave.), which is attractive and secure, is near Madison Square Garden, and has the lowest rates; and **Eastgate Tower** (⊠ 222 E. 39th St.). Except for the contemporary Eastgate and the Art Deco Beekman Tower, all have traditional guest-room decor. Most accommodations have completely equipped pantries; larger units have dining areas with full-size tables. Most properties have restaurants, on-site fitness centers, and coin laundry. ⊠ *Sales office, 500 W. 37th St., 10018,* ☎ *212/465–3600 or 800/637–8483,* ⅏ *212/465–3663. AE, DC, MC, V.*

$$ ⊞ **Gramercy Park Hotel.** This Queen Anne–style hotel is somewhat shabby; rooms have dreary, worn furnishings and old-fashioned baths. Still, it's almost the only hotel in this elegant neighborhood, which boasts the city's least-populated park. The park remains thus because it's locked, but hotel guests can use it. Further advantages to staying here include a bar with a pianist, hot hors d'oeuvres (at happy hour only), and wicked martinis. ⊠ *2 Lexington Ave., 10010,* ☎ *212/475–4320 or 800/221–4083,* ⅏ *212/505–0535. 509 rooms. Restaurant, bar, beauty salon, meeting rooms. AE, D, DC, MC, V.*

$$ ⊞ **Jolly Madison Towers.** The Italian Jolly Hotels chain continually works on this little Murray Hill bargain, with improvements such as glass shower stalls in the tiny bathrooms; fresh carpets and bedspreads in the unobjectionable, if unspectacular, bedrooms; and a good restaurant serving northern Italian cuisine. A separate concession on the premises offers shiatsu massage and Japanese sauna. ⊠ *22 E. 38th St., 10016,* ☎ *212/802–0600 or 800/225–4340,* ⅏ *212/447–0747. 222 rooms. Restaurant, bar, massage, sauna. AE, DC, MC, V.*

$ ⊞ **The Gershwin.** Young, foreign travelers flock to this hip
★ budget hotel, housed in a converted 13-story Greek Revival. Enter, and be visually assaulted by a giant primary-color car-

toony sculpture, one of many works by house artist Brad Howe. Rooms are all painted in custard yellow and kelly green and are somewhat crumbly in places, with no air-conditioning. Dormitories have four or eight beds and a remarkable $22 rate. You won't be spending much time in your room, however, because of all the activities here: band appearances, film series, summer rooftop barbecues in summer, and the like. ⊠ *7 E. 27th St., 10016,* ☎ *212/545–8000,* ℻ *212/684–5546. 160 rooms. Restaurant, bar. MC, V.*

Chelsea, Greenwich Village, SoHo, Chinatown

$$$ 🖭 **SoHo Grand.** SoHo's first hotel has an appropriately
★ high-style aesthetic. Starting from the first floor, the grand, self-suspended staircase of translucent bottle glass and iron recalls the vast, columned interiors and fanciful cast-iron embellishments of the neighborhood's 19th-century buildings. Upstairs in the Grand Salon, 16-ft-high windows and overscaled furniture complement the immense stone pillars that rise from below. Guest rooms have custom-designed furnishings, including drafting-table-style desks, nightstands that mimic sculptors' stands, and minibars made of old campaign chests. In the tavern-style Canal House, superb gourmet renditions of American favorites (macaroni and cheese, crab cakes) are served at surprisingly palatable prices. ⊠ *310 W. Broadway, 10013,* ☎ *212/965–3000 or 800/965–3000,* ℻ *212/965–3244. 367 rooms. Restaurant, bar, exercise room, meeting rooms. AE, D, DC, MC, V.*

$ 🖭 **Larchmont Hotel.** You might miss the entrance to this
★ Beaux Arts brownstone, whose geranium boxes and lanterns blend right in with the old New York feel of West 11th Street. If you don't mind shared bathrooms and no room service or concierge, the residential-style accommodations are all anyone could ask for at this price, which includes Continental breakfast. Rooms have a tasteful safari theme, with rattan furniture, ceiling fans, and framed animal or botanical prints; your own private sink and stocked bookshelf will make you feel right at home. ⊠ *27 W. 11th St., 10011,* ☎ *212/989–9333,* ℻ *212/989–9496. 77 rooms. Breakfast room, kitchen. AE, D, DC, MC, V.*

$ 🖭 **Washington Square Hotel.** This cozy Greenwich Village hotel has a true European feel and style, from the
★

wrought iron and gleaming brass in the small, elegant lobby to the personal attention given by the staff. Rooms are simple but pleasant and well maintained; request one with a window. Continental breakfast is included in the room rate. There's also a good, reasonably priced restaurant, C3. The manager has strong ties to the local jazz community and enjoys providing tips about what's happening at the nearby Blue Note. ✉ *103 Waverly Pl., 10011,* ☎ *212/777–9515 or 800/222–0418,* 𝔽𝔸𝕏 *212/979–8373. 150 rooms. Restaurant, bar, exercise room. AE, MC, V.*

5 Nightlife and the Arts

NIGHTLIFE

Revised by
Anastasia
Mills and
David Low

Okay, so you've taken the Staten Island ferry, you've lunched at the Plaza, visited the Met. But don't tuck yourself in just yet. Get yourself truly attuned to the Big Apple's schedule, which runs more by New York nocturnal than by eastern standard time. Even if you're not a night owl by habit, it's worth staying up late at least once, because by night, Manhattan takes on a whole new identity.

Clubs and Entertainment

For the tattooed and pierced, *Paper* magazine's "P.M. 'Til Dawn" and bar sections have as good a listing as exists of the roving clubs and the best of the fashionable crowd's hangouts. *Time Out New York* offers a comprehensive weekly listing of amusements by category. The more staid Friday *New York Times*'s "Weekend" section carries a "Sounds Around Town" column that can clue you in to what's in the air, as can the *Village Voice*, a weekly newspaper that probably has more nightclub ads than any other rag in the world. The *Village Voice* is now free and disappears from its red kiosks on street corners all over the city often by the afternoon it arrives there (Wednesday). Some newsstands and bookstores also stock it, but you'll have to search pretty hard—it's worth the effort. Or stop by Tower Records (⊠ Broadway and E. 4th St., ☎ 212/505–1500; ⊠ Broadway and W. 66th St., ☎ 212/799–2500), where flyers about coming events and club passes are stacked in the entry. Just remember that events change almost weekly. We've tried to give you a rounded sample of reliable hangouts—but phone ahead to make sure your target nightspot hasn't closed. Most charge a cover, which can range from $2 to $25 or more depending on the club and the night. Take cash, because many places don't accept plastic.

Putting on the Ritz

The Carlyle (⊠ 35 E. 76th St., ☎ 212/744–1600). The hotel's discreetly sophisticated Café Carlyle is where Bobby Short plays when he's in town; otherwise, you might find Barbara Cook or Eartha Kitt purring by a piano. Bemelmans Bar, with murals by the author of the Madeline books, regularly stars pianists Barbara Carroll and Peter Mintun.

Oak Room (✉ Algonquin Hotel, 59 W. 44th St., ☎ 212/840–6800). Though the Algonquin has faded, this room still offers yesteryear's charms. Just head straight for the long, narrow club-cum–watering hole; you might find the hopelessly romantic singer Andrea Marcovicci, or pianist Steve Ross playing Berlin or Porter.

Rainbow Room and **Rainbow & Stars** (✉ 30 Rockefeller Plaza, ☎ 212/632–5000). You can find two kinds of heaven high up on Rockefeller Center's 65th floor. The Rainbow Room serves dinner (☞ Chapter 3) and dancing to the strains of a live orchestra, while at the intimate Rainbow & Stars, classy singers such as Maureen McGovern and Rosemary Clooney entertain.

Supper Club (✉ 240 W. 47th St., ☎ 212/921–1940). This huge, prix-fixe dinner-and-dancing club specializes in cheek-to-cheek big band sounds on Friday and Saturday nights, complete with a full orchestra. You wouldn't recognize it the rest of the week, when touring alternative and rock-and-roll acts like Mazzy Star and the Black Crowes take the stage.

Clubbing

Denim and Diamonds (✉ 511 Lexington Ave., ☎ 212/371–1600). Break out your boots, y'all, and get out on the dance floor for country line dancing every night of the week. If you need help strutting your stuff, come between 7 and 8 PM for lessons. There are two pool tables and a DJ spinning C&W on the main floor; upstairs in the Roadhouse, there's live music Friday and Saturday. Southwestern food is served here, too.

Le Bar Bat (✉ 311 W. 57th St., ☎ 212/307–7228). This bamboo-encrusted, multitiered monster of a club fits right in with the Planet Hollywood on 57th Street's Theme Restaurant Row, but a flashy good time can be had here among the Euro and prepster posers.

Nell's (✉ 246 W. 14th St., ☎ 212/675–1567). Back in vogue, Nell Campbell (of *Rocky Horror* fame) reintroduced sophistication to nightlife with her club. The tone in the upstairs live-music jazz salon is Victorian; downstairs, you can dance to a DJ. The boîte opens at 10 PM and closes at 4 AM nightly.

Robots (✉ 25 Ave. B, ☎ 212/995−0968). So it's 3 AM on a Saturday morning and you're all tanked up with no place to go. Stop in here, where the absence of alcohol from 4 to 9 AM permits patrons to party all night long. Work off that buzz to hip-hop on the dance floor, or nod off in the upstairs lounge.

Roseland (✉ 239 W. 52nd St., ☎ 212/247−0200). This famous old ballroom dance floor is still open for ballroom dancing Thursday (music provided by a DJ) and Sunday (music by a live orchestra and a DJ).

Roxy (✉ 515 W. 18th St., ☎ 212/645−5156). Roller disco on Tuesday and Wednesday, bridge-and-tunnel dance club Friday and Saturday, this huge hall is gay-centric on Tuesday and draws a mixed rave crowd on others.

Webster Hall (✉ 125 E. 11th St., ☎ 212/353−1600). This fave among NYU students and similar species boasts four floors and five eras of music. Go for the live bands on Thursday, the dance DJs on Friday and Saturday—or the trapeze artists any night.

Jazz

Birdland (✉ 315 W. 44th St., ☎ 212/581−3080). From 5 PM to midnight you'll find up-and-coming groups here—plus dinner.

Blue Note (✉ 131 W. 3rd St., ☎ 212/475−8592). Just an average week could bring Spyro Gyra, the Modern Jazz Quartet, and Jon Hendricks. Expect a steep music charge, except on Monday, when record labels promote their artists' new releases for an average ticket price of $7.50.

Cajun (✉ 129 8th Ave., ☎ 212/691−6174). This landlocked Chelsea restaurant with a riverboat feel dishes New Orleans–style jazz alongside Cajun-Creole grub. Live music from the likes of former Louis Armstrong clarinetist Joe Muranyi will make you feel like you've ducked in off Bourbon Street.

Knitting Factory (✉ 74 Leonard St., ☎ 212/219−3055). This eclectic gem of a cross-genre music café in TriBeCa features avant-garde jazz in a homey, funky setting.

Sweet Basil (⊠ 88 7th Ave. S, ☎ 212/242–1785). A little ritzy, though reliable, this nightspot runs from swing to fusion. Sunday brunch (2–6 PM) with trumpeter Doc Cheatham is truly a religious experience.

Village Vanguard (⊠ 178 7th Ave. S, ☎ 212/255–4037). This former Thelonius Monk haunt, the prototype of the old-world jazz club, lives on in a smoky cellar, in which jam the likes of Wynton Marsalis and James Carter.

Rock

Bitter End (⊠ 147 Bleecker St., ☎ 212/673–7030). This old Village standby still serves up its share of new talent; Lisa Loeb, Joan Armatrading, and Warren Zevon once played here. Check before arriving; blues, country, rock, and jazz all make appearances here.

CBGB & OMFUG (⊠ 315 Bowery, ☎ 212/982–4052). American punk rock was born here, in this long, black tunnel of a club featuring bands with inventive names: Shirley Temple of Doom, Trick Babies, and Xanax 25.

Coney Island High (⊠ 15 St. Mark's Pl., ☎ 212/674–7959). Murals of Coney Island amusement-park sideshow acts don't add much cheer to the black and red walls of this hardcore rock haven, which is not nearly as venerable as its state of decrepitude suggests.

Irving Plaza (⊠ 17 Irving Pl., ☎ 212/777–6800 or 212/777–1224 for concert hot line). Looking for Marilyn Manson, the Jesus Lizard, or Better Than Ezra? You'll find them in this perfect-size place for general-admission live music.

Wetlands (⊠ 161 Hudson St., ☎ 212/966–4225). If you can ignore the environmental murals and the hokey broken-down-VW-bus–cum–gift-shop, this hard-to-find club rules, mostly because it draws great, often danceable, often psychedelic bands. Dave Matthews and Hootie and the Blowfish both "developed" here.

World Music

Belmont Lounge (⊠ 117 E. 15th St., ☎ 212/533–0009) Come here Tuesday for classic salsa, mambo, and charanga spun by DJ Frankie Inglese. Perry Farrell and Trent

Reznor have been spotted at this unpretentious, new-in-'96, watering hole and music venue.

Copacabana (⊠ 617 W. 57th St., ☎ 212/582–2672). Music and passion were always in fashion at this legendary nightclub, but now it's in the form of Latin music by such performers as the three Titos: Ruiz, Riojas, and Nieves. Women often pay less, so give a call.

Paddy Reilly's Music Bar (⊠ 519 2nd Ave., ☎ 212/686–1210). Irish rock-and-roots hybrid Black 47 (named for the year of the great famine) has a standing Saturday night gig at this cramped but congenial club. Or stop in on Thursday for a traditional Irish jam session.

SOB's (⊠ 204 Varick St., ☎ 212/243–4940). Since 1982, this has been the—and we mean *the*—place for reggae, Trinidadian carnival, zydeco, African, and especially Latin tunes and salsa rhythms. The initials stand for Sounds of Brazil, just in case you wondered. The decor is à la Tropicana; the favored drink, a Brazilian *caipirinha*.

Blues and Folk

Bottom Line (⊠ 15 W. 4th St., ☎ 212/228–7880). Clubs come and go, but this granddaddy prevails. Its reputation is for showcasing talents on their way up, as it did for both Stevie Wonder and Bruce Springsteen. Recent visitors include Buster Poindexter and Jane Siberry. When a name pulls in a crowd, patrons are packed like a sardine at mostly long, thin tables.

Chicago Blues (⊠ 73 8th Ave., ☎ 212/924–9755). Big Time Sarah, Jimmy Dawkins, the Holmes Brothers, and others have cozied into this nothing-fancy West Village blues club.

Manny's Car Wash (⊠ 1558 3rd Ave., ☎ 212/369–2583). Jams are only on Sunday, but live bands dish up the blues seven nights.

Tramps (⊠ 45 W. 21st St., ☎ 212/727–7788). For more than two decades Tramps has delivered bands like the Dixie Dregs and NRBQ; now it's got Sponge and George Clinton. Come for Chicago blues or most any other kind of music around.

Cabaret

Arcimboldo (✉ 220 E. 46th St., ☎ 212/972–4646). This peachy Italian restaurant dishes out more than spaghetti on Sunday, when it offers its "Opera with Taste" entertainment series, serving up singers from Lincoln Center along with a prix-fixe dinner for a mere $40.

The Duplex (✉ 61 Christopher St., ☎ 212/255–5438). Catch a singing luminary on the rise, a drop-in fresh from Broadway at the open mike, or a comedienne polishing up her act at this longtime Village favorite on Sheridan Square. Opened in 1951, it's New York's oldest continuing cabaret.

Fez (✉ 380 Lafayette St., ☎ 212/533–2680). Tucked away in the trendy Time Café, this Moroccan-themed Casbah offers everything from drag shows to readings and jazz amid a polished young crowd.

Michael's Pub (✉ Parker Meridien Hotel, 118 W. 57th St., ☎ 212/758–2272). Woody Allen often moonlights on the clarinet here on Monday nights when he performs with his New Orleans Jazz Band. Tuesday through Saturday, the Eddie Davis Dixieland Jazz Band has a standing gig. The crowd is very monied, very uptown.

Comedy Clubs

Comedy Cellar (✉ 117 MacDougal St., ☎ 212/254–3480). This spot has been running for 17 years now beneath the Olive Tree Café, with a bill that's a good barometer of who's hot.

Dangerfield's (✉ 1118 1st Ave., ☎ 212/593–1650). Since 1969, this has been an important showcase for prime comic talent. It's owned by comedian Rodney Dangerfield.

New York Comedy Club (✉ 241 E. 24th St., ☎ 212/696–5233). This intimate club, chock-full of comedy memorabilia and talent such as Brett Butler, Colin Quinn, and Damon Wayans, has been referred to as "the Wal-Mart of comedy," as covers are low or nonexistent.

Original Improvisation (✉ 433 W. 34th St., ☎ 212/279–3446). The Improv is to comedy what the Blue Note is to jazz. Lots of now-famous comedians got their first laughs here, among them Richard Pryor.

Bars

Vintage Classics

Algonquin Hotel Lounge (⊠ 59 W. 44th St., ☏ 212/840–6800). This is a venerable spot, not only because it was the site of the fabled literary Round Table but also because it has an elegant tone. (☞ Oak Room *in* Putting on the Ritz, *above.*)

Elaine's (⊠ 1703 2nd Ave., ☏ 212/534–8103). The food's nothing special, and you will be relegated to an inferior table, but go to gawk; try it late, when the stars rise in Elaine's firmament. Woody Allen's favorite table is by the cappuccino machine.

King Cole Bar (⊠ St. Regis Hotel, 2 E. 55th St., ☏ 212/753–4500). The famed Maxwell Parrish mural is a welcome sight at this gorgeous midtown rendezvous spot.

River Café (⊠ 1 Water St., Brooklyn, ☏ 718/522–5200). An eminently romantic spot hidden at the foot of the Brooklyn Bridge, this restaurant offers smashing views of Wall Street and the East River.

Top of the Tower (⊠ Beekman Tower, 3 Mitchell Pl., near 1st Ave. at 49th St., ☏ 212/355–7300). There are higher hotel-top lounges, but this one on the 26th floor still feels halfway to heaven. The atmosphere is elegant and subdued.

"21" Club (⊠ 21 W. 52nd St., ☏ 212/582–7200). Famous for its old-time club atmosphere even before it was filmed in *All About Eve,* this isn't exactly a swinging joint, but its conservative environs evoke a sense of connections, power, and prestige.

Watering Holes

SOHO AND TRIBECA

El Teddy's (⊠ 219 W. Broadway, ☏ 212/941–7070). You can't miss the gigantic Lady Liberty crown out front and the Judy Jetson Goes to Art Camp decor at this former mob haunt. The margaritas (on the rocks, *por favor*) at this enduring TriBeCa bar are phenomenal.

Max Fish (⊠ 178 Ludlow St., ☏ 212/529–3959). This crowded, grungy kitsch palace on an artsy East Village strip has a twisted image of a grimacing Julio Iglesias over the bar and a pool table in back. Downtown mainstays like the Ramones have been spotted here.

Naked Lunch (✉ 17 Thompson St., ☎ 212/343–0828). Dazzlingly successful, this Burroughs-inspired, earth-tone SoHo haunt is said to be often graced by Robert De Niro, among others.

Sporting Club (✉ 99 Hudson St., ☎ 212/219–0900). The six 10-ft screens and 11 TV monitors here stay tuned to the evening's major sports event. Aficionados come in after punching out on Wall Street.

Spy (✉ 101 Greene St., ☎ 212/343–9000). Part of the lounge trend going on in Manhattan at press time, Spy celebrated its first birthday in 1996 with a celebrity-filled bash. Settle into a plush couch and enjoy the baroque parlor setting and pretty people.

CHELSEA AND THE VILLAGE

Chumley's (✉ 86 Bedford St., ☎ 212/675–4449). There's no sign to help you find this place—they took it down during Chumley's speakeasy days—but when you reach the corner of Barrow Street, you're very close. A fireplace warms this relaxed spot, where the burgers are hearty and the clientele collegiate.

Flight 151 (✉ 151 8th Ave., ☎ 212/229–1868). This popular, unpretentious neighborhood hangout serves lunch, dinner, and a bargain all-you-can-eat brunch on weekends. The polished wood bar, candlelit booths, and friendly staff create a welcoming atmosphere.

McSorley's Old Ale House (✉ 15 E. 7th St., ☎ 212/473–9148). One of New York's oldest saloons (opened in 1854), this is a must-see for first-timers to Gotham.

Peculier Pub (✉ 145 Bleecker St., ☎ 212/353–1327). Here, in the heart of the Village, you'll find nearly 400 brands of beer, from Anchor Steam to Zywiec.

White Horse Tavern (✉ 567 Hudson St., ☎ 212/989–3956). Here's where Dylan Thomas drained his last cup. In warm weather, there's outdoor café drinking.

Bowery Bar (✉ 358 Bowery, ☎ 212/475–2220). Long lines peer through venetian blinds at the fabulous crowd within. If the bouncer says there's a private party going on, more likely than not, it's his way of turning you away nicely.

Café Tabac (✉ 232 E. 9th St., ☎ 212/674–7072). Practice your glare before entering the ground-floor lounge of this pretentious salon, the site of many Madonna visits as well as fights between Christian Slater, Ethan Hawke, and whichever models they are dating at the moment.

Lucky Cheng's (✉ 24 1st Ave., ☎ 212/473–0516). Have a bite beside the goldfish pond downstairs, or mingle amid the gilt and leopard and be served by lovely waiters and bartenders in drag at this Pacific Rim restaurant–cum–cross-dressing cabaret .

Old Town Bar and Restaurant (✉ 45 E. 18th St., ☎ 212/529–6732). Proudly unpretentious, this watering hole is heavy on the mahogany and redolent of "old New York." True to its name, the Old Town has been around since 1892.

Republic (✉ 37 Union Sq. W, ☎ 212/627–7172). This trendy noodle shop right on Union Square has an elegant and active bar up front. The concept took on so well that at press time, two more Republics were scheduled to open in Manhattan.

Temple Bar (✉ 332 Lafayette St., ☎ 212/925–4242). Romantic and upscale, this unmarked haunt is famous for its martinis and is a treat at any price.

Halcyon Bar (✉ Rihga Royal Hotel, 151 W. 54th St., ☎ 212/307–5000). A big, airy restaurant and bar, Halcyon has large and well-spaced tables and is great for a private chat.

Landmark Tavern (✉ 626 11th Ave., ☎ 212/757–8595). This aged redbrick pub (opened in 1868) is blessed by the glow of warming fireplaces on each of its three floors.

The Royalton (✉ 44 W. 44th St., ☎ 212/768–5000 or 212/869–4400). If you can't find an open seating area in the lobby of this modernistic, Phillipe Starck–designed hotel, search for the tiny, very cool Vodka Bar.

Sardi's (✉ 234 W. 44th St., ☎ 212/221–8440). "The theater is certainly not what it was," croons a cat in *Cats*—and he could be referring to this venerable spot as well. Still, if you care for the theater, don't leave New York without visiting this establishment.

The Whiskey (✉ Paramount Hotel, 235 W. 46th St., ☎ 212/764–5500). Small, dark, and crowded, the Whiskey nevertheless remains a favorite Times Square area bar among hipsters. It's hard to find; look for the potted plants outside.

EAST SIDE

P. J. Clarke's (✉ 915 3rd Ave., ☎ 212/759–1650). New York's most famous Irish bar, this establishment comes complete with the requisite mirrors and polished wood. Lots of after-workers like unwinding here, in a place that recalls the days of Tammany Hall.

Polo Lounge and Restaurant (✉ Westbury Hotel, 840 Madison Ave., ☎ 212/439–4835). This place is, in a word, classy; it's frequented by European royalty and Knickerbocker New York.

UPPER WEST SIDE

China Club (✉ 2130 Broadway, ☎ 212/877–1166). If you don't spot someone famous here within 30 minutes, you just aren't trying hard enough. On Monday night it's the place to be on the Upper West Side.

Iridium (✉ 48 W. 63rd St., ☎ 212/582–2121). The owners spent untold sums to make this lavish restaurant and jazz club near Lincoln Center stand out, which it does. If nothing else, take a look inside for an eyeful of Gaudíesque construction.

O'Neal's Lincoln Center (✉ 49 W. 64th St., ☎ 212/787–4663). Mike O'Neal, the owner of the beloved but now defunct Ginger Man, has moved the bar from that establishment down the street and created a series of rooms (one with a fireplace) serving good pub food.

Gay and Lesbian Bars

DANCE CLUBS AND PARTIES

Clit Club (✉ Mother, 432 W. 14th St., ☎ 212/366–5680). Leather-vested and well-pierced Harley dykes as well as lipstick lesbians dance Friday night away. Call first, because this club roves.

Her/She Bar (✉ 229 W. 28th St., ☎ 212/631–1093). Dance with drag kings every Friday in the self-proclaimed "nation's largest dance club for women."

Jackie 60 (✉ Mother, 432 W. 14th St., 212/366–5680). The gay-friendly house dance party on Tuesday is so hip, there's a hot line (☎ 212/929–6060) that announces the theme of the week so you don't feel left out.

MEN'S BARS

Crowbar (✉ 339 E. 10th St., ☎ 212/228–4448). Gay grungers and NYU students mingle happily at this East Village hot spot, which is especially sizzling on Friday.

Stonewall (✉ 53 Christopher St., ☎ 212/463–0950). With its odd mix of tourists chasing down gay history and down-to-earth locals, the scene is everything but trendy.

The Townhouse (✉ 236 E. 58th St., ☎ 212/754–4649). On good nights it's like stepping into a Brooks Brothers catalog—cashmere sweaters, Rolex watches, distinguished-looking gentlemen—and it's surprisingly festive.

The Works (✉ 428 Columbus Ave., ☎ 212/799–7365). Whether it's Thursday's $1 margarita party or just a regular Upper West Side afternoon, the crowd is usually J. Crew–style or disco hangover at this bar, which has been around for nearly two decades.

WOMEN'S BARS

Crazy Nanny's (✉ 21 7th Ave. S, ☎ 212/366–6312). The crowd is wide-ranging—from urban chic to shaved head—and tends toward the young and the wild. Wednesday and Friday find the crowd grooving to a house DJ while Thursday is C&W line-dancing night.

Julie's (✉ 204 E. 58th St., ☎ 212/688–1294). Popular with the sophisticated-lady, upper-crust crowd, this brownstone basement has a piano bar—and dancing on Sunday and Wednesday nights.

Shescapes (✉ Various locations, ☎ 212/686–5665). This roving dance party is probably the most popular of Manhattan's lesbian soirées.

THE ARTS

New York has somewhere between 200 and 250 legitimate theaters, and many more ad hoc venues—parks, churches, universities, museums, lofts, galleries, streets, and rooftops—where performances ranging from Shakespeare to sword-dancing take place. The city is, as well, a revolving door of festivals and special events: Summer jazz, one-act-play marathons, international film series, and musical celebrations from the classical to the avant-garde are just a few.

Getting Tickets

Prices for **tickets** in New York, especially for Broadway shows, never seem to stop rising. Major concerts and recitals, however, can be equally expensive. The top Broadway ticket prices for musicals are $75; the best seats for nonmusicals can cost as much as $65.

On the positive side, tickets for New York City's arts events usually aren't too hard to come by—unless, of course, you're dead set on seeing the season's hottest sold-out show. Generally, a theater or concert hall's box office is the best place to buy tickets, since in-house ticket sellers make it their business to know about their theaters and shows and don't mind pointing out (on a chart) where you'll be seated. It's always a good idea to purchase tickets in advance to avoid disappointment, especially if you're traveling a long distance. For advance purchase, send the theater or hall a certified check or money order, several alternate dates, and a self-addressed, stamped envelope.

You can also pull out a credit card and call **Tele-charge** (☎ 212/239–6200) or **TicketMaster** (☎ 212/307–4100) to reserve tickets for Broadway and Off-Broadway shows—newspaper ads generally will specify which you should use for any given event. Both services will give you seat locations over the phone upon request. A surcharge ($2–$5.50 per ticket) will be added to the total in addition to a $2.50 handling fee. You can arrange to have your tickets mailed to you or have them waiting for you at the theater.

You may be tempted to buy from ticket scalpers. But beware: They have reportedly sold tickets to the big hits for up to $200 when seats were still available at the box office for much less. Bear in mind that ticket scalping is against the law in New York. Also, these scalpers may even sell you phony tickets.

Off- and Off-Off-Broadway theaters have their own joint box office called **Ticket Central** (✉ 416 W. 42nd St., ☎ 212/279–4200). It's open daily between 1 and 8 PM. Although there are no discounts here, tickets to performances in these theaters are usually less expensive than Broadway tickets, and they cover an array of events, including legitimate theater, performance art, and dance.

Discount Tickets

The **TKTS booth** in Duffy Square (✉ 47th St. and Broadway, ☎ 212/768–1818) is New York's best-known discount source. TKTS sells day-of-performance tickets for Broadway and Off-Broadway plays at discounts that, depending on a show's popularity, often go as low as 50% to 75% of the usual price, plus a $2.50 surcharge per ticket. The names of shows available on that day are posted on electronic boards in front of the booth. If you're interested in a Wednesday or Saturday matinee, go to the booth between 10 and 2, check out what's offered, and then wait in line. For evening performances, the booth is open 3–8; for Sunday matinee and evening performances, noon–8. *Note: TKTS accepts only cash or traveler's checks—no credit cards.*

So successful has TKTS proved that an auxiliary booth operates in the Wall Street area (✉ 2 World Trade Center mezzanine). The World Trade Center branch is open weekdays 11–5:30, Saturday 11–3:30. For matinees and Sundays, you have to purchase tickets the day before the performance. The lines at the downtown TKTS booth are usually shorter than those at Duffy Square, though the uptown booth usually has a larger selection of plays.

Some Broadway and Off-Broadway shows sell reduced-price tickets for performances scheduled before opening night. Look at newspaper ads for discounted previews, or consult the box office. Tickets may cost less at matinees, particularly on Wednesday.

Finding Out What's On

To find out who or what's playing where, your first stop should be the newsstand. The **New York Times** comes in pretty handy, especially on Friday, with its "Weekend" section. The **New Yorker** magazine has long been known for its discerning and often witty listings called "Goings On About Town"—a section at the front of the magazine that contains ruthlessly succinct reviews of theater, dance, art, music, film, and nightlife. **New York** magazine's "Cue" listings are extremely helpful, covering everything from art to the written word.

For adventurous, more unconventional tastes, consult **Time Out New York,** a comprehensive guide to all kinds of entertainment happenings around town, with particularly good coverage of the downtown scene. The free weekly newspaper the **Village Voice** is a lively information source; its club listings and "Choices" section are both reliable.

NYC/ON STAGE (☎ 212/768–1818) is the Theatre Development Fund's 24-hour information service.

Theater

To most people, New York theater means **Broadway,** that region bounded by 42nd and 53rd streets, between 6th and 9th avenues, where bright, transforming lights shine upon porn theaters and jewel-box playhouses alike. Within the past three years, several **42nd Street houses** have come back to life. The **New Victory** (✉ 209 W. 42nd St.), previously known as the Theater Republic and the Belasco Theater, is the oldest surviving playhouse in New York; reopened in 1995 and now completely modernized, it stages exciting productions for kids. The **Ford Center for the Performing Arts** (✉ 213–215 42nd St.), a lavish 1,839-seat theater constructed on the site of two classic houses, the Lyric and the Apollo, incorporates original architectural elements from both theaters, along with state-of-the-art facilities to accommodate grand-scale musical shows. Across the street, the Walt Disney Company has refurbished the Art Nouveau **New Amsterdam** (✉ 214 W. 42nd St.); Eddie Cantor, Will Rogers, Fanny Brice, and the Ziegfeld Follies once drew crowds here.

Not all that long ago it was relatively simple to categorize the New York stage beyond Broadway. It was divided into **Off-Broadway** and **Off-Off-Broadway,** depending on a variety of factors that included theatrical contract type, location, and ticket price. Today such distinctions seem strained, as Off-Broadway prices have risen and the quality of some Off-Off-Broadway productions has decidedly improved. Off- and Off-Off-Broadway is where Eric Bogosian, Ann Magnuson, John Leguizamo, Danny Hoch, and Laurie Anderson make their home and where *Driving Miss Daisy, Steel Magnolias,* and *Jeffrey* were first conceived. Attendance and ticket sales remain relatively healthy, proving how vital this segment of the theater world is to New York culture.

One of the major Off-Broadway enclaves is **Theatre Row,** a collection of small houses (100 seats or fewer)—such as the **John Houseman Theatre** (⊠ 450 W. 42nd St., ☎ 212/967–9077), the **Douglas Fairbanks Theatre** (⊠ 432 W. 42nd St., ☎ 212/239–4321), and **Playwrights Horizons** (⊠ 416 W. 42nd St., ☎ 212/279–4200)—on the downtown side of 42nd Street between 9th and 10th avenues. Downtown in the East Village, the **Joseph Papp Public Theater** (⊠ 425 Lafayette St., ☎ 212/260–2400) mounts new and classic plays, along with dance concerts, literary readings, and musical events. **Greenwich Village,** around Sheridan Square, is another Off-Broadway neighborhood.

Many estimable **Off-Broadway theaters** are flung across the Manhattan map: the **Astor Place Theatre** (⊠ 434 Lafayette St., ☎ 212/254–4370); the **Orpheum Theatre** (⊠ 126 2nd Ave., at 8th St., ☎ 212/477–2477); the **Variety Arts Theatre** (⊠ 110 3rd Ave., at 14th St., ☎ 212/239–6200); the **Union Square Theatre** (⊠ 100 E. 17th St., ☎ 212/505–0700); the **American Place Theatre** (⊠ 111 W. 46th St., ☎ 239–6200); the **Lamb's Theatre** (⊠ 130 W. 44th St., ☎ 212/997–1780); the **Triad Theatre** (⊠ 158 W. 72nd St., ☎ 212/799–4599); and the **Promenade Theatre** (⊠ Broadway at 76th St., ☎ 212/580–1313).

Dance

Ballet

The **New York City Ballet (NYCB),** a hallmark troupe for nearly 50 years, performs in Lincoln Center's **New York State Theater** (☎ 212/870–5570). Its winter season runs from mid-November through February—with the beloved annual production of *George Balanchine's The Nutcracker* ushering in the December holiday season—while its spring season lasts from late April through June.

Across the plaza at Lincoln Center, the **Metropolitan Opera House** (☎ 212/362–6000) is home to the **American Ballet Theatre,** renowned for its brilliant renditions of the great 19th-century classics (*Swan Lake, Giselle, The Sleeping Beauty,* and *La Bayardère*) as well as for the unique scope of its eclectic contemporary repertoire. Since its inception in 1940, the company has included some of the greatest dancers of the century, such as Mikhail Baryshnikov, Natalia Makarova, Rudolf Nureyev, Gelsey Kirkland, and Cynthia Gregory. Its New York season runs from April to June.

Modern Dance

At **City Center** (✉ 131 W. 55th St., ☎ 212/581–1212), the moderns hold sway. In seasons past, the **Alvin Ailey Dance Company, Twyla Tharp and Dancers,** the **Martha Graham Dance Company,** the **Paul Taylor Dance Company,** the **Dance Theater of Harlem,** and the **Merce Cunningham Dance Company** have performed here. The **Brooklyn Academy of Music** (✉ 30 Lafayette Ave., ☎ 718/636–4100) features both American and foreign contemporary dance troupes as part of its **Next Wave Festival** every fall.

A growing international modern-dance center is the **Joyce Theater** (✉ 175 8th Ave., ☎ 212/242–0800), housed in a former Art Deco movie theater. Recent featured companies have included the startling **Parsons Dance Company,** the lyrical **Lar Lubovitch Dance Company,** the passionate **Ballet Hispanico,** and the fantastical **Momix** troupe. The Joyce has an eclectic program, including tap, jazz, ballroom, and ethnic dance, and it often showcases emerging choreographers.

Manhattan has several other small-scale, mostly experimental and avant-garde dance forums:

Dance Theater Workshop (✉ 219 W. 19th St., ☎ 212/924–0077) serves as one of New York's most successful laboratories for new dance.

Merce Cunningham Studio (✉ 55 Bethune St., ☎ 212/691–9751) showcases performances by cutting-edge modern dance companies.

PS 122 (✉ 150 1st Ave., at 9th St., ☎ 212/477–5288) programs dance events that often border on performance art.

Tribeca Performing Arts Center (✉ 199 Chambers St., ☎ 212/346–8510) presents dance troupes from around the world.

Music

Classical Music

Lincoln Center (✉ W. 62nd to 66th Sts., Columbus to Amsterdam Aves.) remains the city's musical nerve center, especially when it comes to the classics.

The **New York Philharmonic** (☎ 212/875–5656), led by Music Director Kurt Masur, performs at Avery Fisher Hall from late September to early June. In addition to its magical concerts, the Philharmonic also schedules weeknight Rush Hour Concerts at 6:45 PM and Casual Saturdays Concerts at 2 PM; these special events, offered throughout the season, last one hour and are priced lower than the regular subscription concerts.

Near Avery Fisher is **Alice Tully Hall** (✉ Broadway at 65th St., ☎ 212/875–5050), an intimate "little white box," considered as acoustically perfect as concert houses get. Here you can listen to the **Chamber Music Society of Lincoln Center,** promising Juilliard students, chamber music ensembles, music on period instruments, choral music, famous soloists, and concert groups. Lincoln Center's outdoor **Damrosch Park** and nearby **Bruno Walter Auditorium** (in the Library of the Performing Arts, ☎ 212/870–1630) often offer free concerts.

While Lincoln Center is only some 30 years old, another famous classical music palace—**Carnegie Hall** (✉ W. 57th St. at 7th Ave., ☎ 212/247–7800)—recently celebrated its 100th birthday. This is the place where the great pianist

Paderewski was attacked by ebullient crowds (who claimed kisses and locks of his hair) after a performance in 1891; where young Leonard Bernstein, standing in for New York Philharmonic conductor Bruno Walter, made his triumphant debut in 1943; where Jack Benny and Isaac Stern fiddled together; and where the Beatles played one of their first U.S. concerts. When threats of the wrecker's ball loomed large in 1960, a consortium of Carnegie loyalists (headed by Isaac Stern) rose to save it; a multimillion-dollar renovation in 1986 worked cosmetic wonders.

Other prime classical music locales around the city include:

Bargemusic at the Fulton Ferry Landing in Brooklyn (☎ 718/624–4061) keeps chamber-music groups busy year-round on an old barge with a fabulous skyline view.

Grace Rainey Rogers Auditorium at the Metropolitan Museum of Art (⊠ 5th Ave. at 82nd St., ☎ 212/570–3949) offers performances of classical music in stately surroundings.

Merkin Concert Hall at the Abraham Goodman House (⊠ 129 W. 67th St., ☎ 212/550–3330) is almost as prestigious for performers as the concert halls at Lincoln Center.

Outdoor Concerts

Weather permitting, the city presents myriad musical events in the great outdoors. Each August, the plaza around Lincoln Center explodes with the **Lincoln Center Out-of-Doors** (☎ 212/875–5108) series. In the summertime, both the **Metropolitan Opera** and the **New York Philharmonic** appear in municipal parks to play free concerts (for information call Lincoln Center, ☎ 212/875–5400, or the City Parks Special Events Hotline, ☎ 212/360–3456). **Central Park SummerStage** (⊠ Rumsey Playfield, Central Park at 72nd St., ☎ 212/360–2777 or 800/201–7275) presents free music programs, ranging from world music to alternative rock, generally on Saturday and Sunday afternoons from June through August. The **Museum of Modern Art** hosts free Friday and Saturday evening concerts of 20th-century music in its sculpture garden as part of the **Summergarden** series (☎ 212/708–9480), held from mid-June through August.

Opera

Recent decades have sharply intensified the public's appreciation of grand opera—partly because of the charismatic personalities of such great singers as Luciano Pavarotti, Placido Domingo, and Cecilia Bartoli and partly because of the efforts of New York's magnetic **Metropolitan Opera** (☎ 212/362–6000). Its vaunted repertoire can be heard from October to mid-April, and though tickets can cost more than $100, many less expensive seats and standing room are available—some 600 seats are sold at $24; bear in mind that weekday prices are slightly lower than weekend prices. Standing-room tickets for the week's performances go on sale on Saturday.

The **New York City Opera,** which performs from September through November and in March and April at Lincoln Center's **New York State Theater** (☎ 212/870–5570), continues its tradition of a diverse repertoire, consisting of adventurous and rarely seen works as well as beloved classic opera and operetta favorites. The company maintains its ingenious practice of "supertitling"—electronically displaying, above the stage, line-by-line English translations of foreign-language operas.

Opera aficionados should also keep track of the **Carnegie Hall** (☎ 212/247–7800) schedule for debuting singers and performances by the **Opera Orchestra of New York** (✉ Box 1226, 10023, ☎ 212/799–1982), which specializes in rarely performed operas, often performed by star soloists. Pay close attention to provocative opera offerings at the **Brooklyn Academy of Music** (☎ 718/636–4100), which often premieres avant-garde works difficult to see elsewhere.

Film and Video

For information on first-run movie schedules and theaters, dial 212/777–3456, the **MovieFone** sponsored by WNEW 102.7 FM and the *New York Times.* You can also call this number to order tickets in advance with a credit card; not all movie theaters participate, however, and the surcharge is $1.50 per ticket.

Museums

In midtown Manhattan, the **Museum of Television and Radio** (✉ 25 W. 52nd St., ☎ 212/621–6800) has a gigantic collection of more than 75,000 radio and TV shows, from the golden past to the present. The museum's library provides 96 consoles where you can watch or listen to whatever you wish for up to two hours at a time. The museum also schedules theater screenings, gallery exhibits, and series for children.

Especially for Kids

Madison Square Garden (⊠ 7th Ave., between 31st and 33rd Sts., ☎ 212/465–6000) offers, besides sports events, some Disney and Sesame Street extravaganzas. There are major ice shows in winter, and each spring brings the **Ringling Bros. and Barnum & Bailey Circus** (check local newspapers for dates, times, and ticket information). The **Big Apple Circus** (⊠ 35 W. 35th St., ☎ 212/268–0055) charms the toughest New Yorkers in locations all over the city during spring and summer and is in residence at Lincoln Center from October through January.

Theater

New Victory Theater (⊠ 209 W. 42nd St., ☎ 212/239–6255), the oldest surviving theater in New York, now presents a variety of plays and performances devoted solely to families. **Paper Bag Players** (⊠ Sylvia and Danny Kaye Playhouse, 68th St., between Park and Lexington Aves., ☎ 212/772–4448) is the longest-running children's theater group in the nation. **Marionette Theater** (⊠ Swedish Cottage, Central Park at W. 81st St., ☎ 212/988–9093) features programs Tuesday–Saturday.

FILM

Several museums sponsor special film programs aimed at families and children, including the Museum of Modern Art and the Museum of Television and Radio (☞ Rockefeller Center and Vicinity *in* Chapter 2). At the **Sony IMAX Theater** (⊠ 1998 Broadway, at 68th St., ☎ 212/336–5000) audience members strap on high-tech headgear that makes nature and specially created feature films appear in 3-D.

6 Shopping

THERE'S SOMETHING FOR EVERYONE in every price range in New York. Fancy a pair of official spoons salvaged from the Kremlin vaults? Just call the **Sovietski Collection** (☎ 800/442–0002). A selection of skulls? **Danse Macabre** (☎ 212/219–3907) downtown can outfit you nicely. Or if you favor high-end designers (especially Italian), the recent store openings along Madison Avenue will keep your credit cards busy. One of Manhattan's biggest shopping lures is the bargain—a temptation fueled in recent years by the Manhattan openings of discount divas such as Loehmann's. Hawkers of not-so-real Gucci watches are stationed at street intersections (even on Madison Avenue), and Canal Street is lined with faux Prada backpacks. There are thrift shops where well-known socialites send their castoffs and movie stars snap up antique lace; although resale prices are definitely higher than in smaller cities, the sheer selection can make up for it. Designers' showroom sales allow you to buy cheap at the source; auctions promise good prices as well.

Revised by Jennifer J. Paull

Shopping Neighborhoods

South Street Seaport

The Seaport's shops are located along the cobbled, pedestrian-only extension to Fulton Street; in the Fulton Market building, the original home of the city's fish market; and on the three levels of Pier 17. Stores in this area tend toward the conservative upscale; for dependable women's clothing try **Ann Taylor** and **Liz Claiborne.** The big catalog house **J. Crew** opened its first Manhattan retail outlet in one of the Seaport's old waterfront hotels. Pier 17 has few surprises, but there are some few-of-a-kind shops, including the **Mark Reuben Gallery** for hand printed sepia-toned photographs of both modern and old-time subjects (heavy on the Yankees).

World Financial Center

Although the nearby World Trade Center bills its concourse as the city's busiest shopping center, the World Financial Center in Battery Park City is also a shopping destination to reckon with, thanks to stores such as **Bar-**

neys New York for clothing and **Godiva Chocolatier** for chocolates. **Quest Toys** has a wonderful selection of wooden and educational playthings.

Lower East Side/East Village

Once home to millions of Jewish immigrants from Russia and Eastern Europe, the Lower East Side is New Yorkers' bargain beat. The center of it all is narrow, unprepossessing Orchard Street, which is crammed with tiny, no-nonsense clothing and shoe stores ranging from kitschy to elegant. Sunday is the busiest day of the week (on Saturday shops in the Orchard Street area are closed). Essential stops include **Fine & Klein** for handbags and **Forman's** for women's clothing. Grand Street (off Orchard Street, south of Delancey Street) is chockablock with linens, towels, and other items for the home; the Bowery (between Grand Street and Delancey Street), with lamps and lighting fixtures. The East Village offers diverse, off-beat specialty stops, including **Little Rickie** for collectible kitsch.

SoHo

The mallification of SoHo has become increasingly evident. Chain stores such as **Victoria's Secret** and **Eddie Bauer** now have Broadway addresses, and **J. Crew** has an outpost on Prince Street. However, there's still a strong percentage of unique shops such as **Miu Miu** for fashion; **Wolfman-Gold & Good Company** for decorative items; **Dean & DeLuca,** a gourmet food emporium; **Zona** and **Moss,** full of well-designed home furnishings and gifts; **Williams-Sonoma Grande Cuisine** for kitchenware and gourmet specialties; and the remarkable **Enchanted Forest** toy store. Many stores in SoHo are open seven days a week.

Lower 5th Avenue/Chelsea

Fifth Avenue south of 23rd Street, along with the streets fanning east and west, is home to a lively downtown crowd. Many of the locals sport clothes from the neighborhood—a mix of the hip like **Emporio Armani, Paul Smith,** and **Matsuda** (for Japanese designer clothing) as well as discount clothiers such as **Moe Ginsburg.** On 6th Avenue are a cluster of superstores, including **Barnes & Noble, T. J. Maxx, Filene's Basement, Burlington Coat Factory,** and **Old Navy,** as well as the colossal **Bed, Bath & Beyond.**

Barneys New York, **2**

Bergdorf Goodman, **3**

Bloomingdale's, **1**

Century 21, **12**

Henri Bendel, **4**

Lord & Taylor, **8**

Lower East Side (Orchard Street), **10**

Macy's, **9**

Rockefeller Center, **6**

Saks Fifth Avenue, **7**

South Street Seaport, **11**

Trump Tower, **5**

World Financial Center, **14**

World Trade Center, **13**

Manhattan Shopping Highlights

Herald Square

Reasonable prices prevail at this intersection of 34th Street and Avenue of the Americas (6th Avenue). Giant **Macy's** has traditionally been the linchpin. Opposite is Manhattan's first **Toys 'R' Us.** Next door on 6th Avenue, the seven-story Manhattan Mall is anchored by **Stern's** department store, which makes for wonderful browsing.

5th Avenue

The boulevard that was once home to some of the biggest names in New York retailing may have lost some ground to neighboring Madison Avenue, but 5th Avenue from Central Park South to Rockefeller Center still has the goods. Strong proof lies in the luster of the multistory **Versace** store, opened in late August 1996—not to mention the renovation of the **Bergdorf Goodman Men** store (at 58th St.) and **Salvatore Ferragamo**'s expansion. The perennial favorites will eat up a lot of shoe leather: **F.A.O. Schwarz** and **Bergdorf Goodman** (at 58th St.); **Tiffany** and **Bulgari** jewelers (at 57th St.); **Ferragamo** and other various luxury stores in **Trump Tower** (at 56th St.); **Steuben** crystal (at 56th St.); **Henri Bendel,** across the street; **Takashimaya** (at 54th St.); **Cartier** jewelers (at 52nd St.); and so on down to the flag-bedecked **Saks Fifth Avenue** (at 50th St.). **Rockefeller Center** itself provides plenty of smaller specialty shops.

57th Street

The short section of 57th Street between 5th and Madison is no longer limited to top-echelon fashion houses, as more affordable (and sizable) stores have muscled their way in. The cartoon-crammed **Warner Bros. Studio Store** finished a massive expansion in fall 1996; not to be outdone, **Nike-Town** has opened the largest of its high-tech U.S. sportswear emporiums. Exclusive stores such as **Chanel, Burberrys, Escada,** and **Hermès** have closed ranks on the north side of the street; when an **Original Levi's Store** opened next to Chanel a couple of years ago, the grande dame of couture edged a few doors closer to Madison Avenue, opening a lofty town house in 1996.

Columbus Avenue

Between 66th and 86th streets, this former tenement district is now home to a rich shopping strip. Stores are mostly modern in design, upscale but not top-of-the-line. Cloth-

ing runs the gamut from traditional for men and women
(**Frank Stella Ltd.**) to high funk (**Betsey Johnson**) and high
style (**Charivari**).

Upper East Side

Madison Avenue, roughly between 57th and 79th streets,
can satisfy almost any couture craving. The magnetic center has shifted a bit in the past year, ratcheting down a few
blocks toward the pull of **Giorgio Armani** (at 65th St.), whose
spacious new digs opened in fall 1996. Other Italian design houses are **Moschino, Valentino, Prada,** and the less
familiar but tantalizing **Etro.** A Gianni Versace **Versus** boutique was slated to open in late 1997 next to his men's and
women's stores. The industrial-edged **Diesel Superstore**
has its first sizable U.S. location at Lexington and 60th Street.
Relative old-timers such as **Coach** have freshened up their
long-run establishments. Madison isn't just a fashion fun-
nel, however; there are several outstanding antiques and
art dealers as well.

Department Stores

ABC Carpet & Home (⊠ 888 Broadway, at 19th St., ☎
212/473–3000). With its recently expanded home decoration
selection, this immense emporium just gets bigger and better. From vintage tea sets to trimmings to meditation cush-
ions, good taste prevails.

Barneys New York (⊠ 660 Madison Ave., at 61st St., ☎
212/826–8900; ⊠ World Financial Center, ☎ 212/945–
1600). The extensive menswear selection is introducing a
handful of edgier designers such as Alexander McQueen.
(Made-to-measure is always available.) The women's department is a showcase of cachet names like Armani, Jil
Sander, and Vivienne Westwood.

Bergdorf Goodman (⊠ 754 5th Ave., between 57th and 58th
Sts., ☎ 212/753–7300). Good taste reigns in an elegant
and understated setting; you can visit the salon in the former Goodman family penthouse apartment. The home department has rooms full of wonderful linens, tableware, and
gifts. The expanded men's store, across the street, is the perfect companion.

Bloomingdale's (✉ 1000 3rd Ave., at 59th St., ☎ 212/355–5900). Only a handful of department stores occupy an entire city block; Macy's is one, and this New York institution is another. Selections are dazzling at all but the lowest price points, and the markdowns on designer goods can be rewarding.

Henri Bendel (✉ 712 5th Ave., between 55th and 56th Sts., ☎ 212/247–1100). Bendel's continues to charm with its stylish displays and its Lalique windows, even as it temporarily discombobulates the uninitiated with its swirling floor plan. Shoe lovers should be forewarned that there is no true footwear department.

Lord & Taylor (✉ 424 5th Ave., between 38th and 39th Sts., ☎ 212/391–3344). This store can be relied upon for the wearable, the fashionable, and the classic in clothes and accessories for women. It's refined, well stocked, and never overwhelming.

Macy's (✉ Herald Sq., Broadway at 34th St., ☎ 212/695–4400). There's a concentration on the mainstream rather than the luxe, and the main floor is reassuringly traditional. For cooking gear and housewares, the freshened-up Cellar nearly outdoes Zabar's.

Saks Fifth Avenue (✉ 611 5th Ave., between 49th and 50th Sts., ☎ 212/753–4000). This wonderful store still embodies the spirit of service and style with which it opened in 1926. Saks believes in good manners, the ceremonies of life . . . and dressing for the part.

Stern's (✉ 33rd St. and 6th Ave., ☎ 212/244–6060). What was the old Gimbel's, a block south of Macy's, lives again as home to an atrium mall, whose nine floors are anchored by Stern's, which is working hard to become as well established here as in the outer boroughs.

Takashimaya New York (✉ 693 5th Ave., between 54th and 55th Sts., ☎ 212/350–0100). This pristine branch of Japan's largest department store carries stylish clothes and fine household items, all of which reflect a combination of Eastern and Western designs. The gardening-section–cum–front-window-display is one of 5th Avenue's most refreshing sights.

Specialty Shops

Antiques

Manhattan Art & Antiques Center (⊠ 1050 2nd Ave., between 55th and 56th Sts., ☎ 212/355–4400). Some 100 dealers stocking everything from paisley and Judaica to satsuma, scientifica, and samovars jumble the three floors here at digestible prices.

Metropolitan Arts and Antiques Pavilion (⊠ 110 W. 19th St., between 6th Ave. and 7th Aves., ☎ 212/463–0200). Good for costume jewelry, offbeat bric-a-brac, and '50s kitsch, this antiques mall holds regularly scheduled auctions and specialty shows featuring rare books, photography, tribal art, Victoriana, and other lots.

Newel Art Galleries (⊠ 425 E. 53rd St., ☎ 212/758–1970). Located near the East Side's interior-design district, this gallery, the city's biggest antiques store, has a huge collection that roams from the Renaissance to the 20th century.

Art Galleries

Gagosian (⊠ 980 Madison Ave., 6th floor, between 76th and 77th Sts., ☎ 212/744–2313; ⊠ 136 Wooster St., between W. Houston and Prince Sts., ☎ 212/228–2828). Works on display are by such established artists as Richard Serra, Willem de Kooning, and Jasper Johns.

Hirschl & Adler (⊠ 21 E. 70th St., ☎ 212/535–8810). A respected dealer of American painting and sculpture, this gallery also offers American decorative arts. Among the celebrated artists whose works are featured: Thomas Cole, Childe Hassam, Ralston Crawford, John Storrs, and William Merritt Chase.

Margo Feiden Galleries (⊠ 699 Madison Ave., between 62nd and 63rd Sts., ☎ 212/677–5330). The specialty here is drawings by theatrical caricaturist Al Hirschfeld, who has been delighting readers of the *New York Times* for more than 60 years.

Books

Gotham Book Mart (⊠ 41 W. 47th St., ☎ 212/719–4448). The late Frances Steloff opened this store years ago with just $200 in her pocket, half of it on loan. But she helped launch James Joyce's *Ulysses,* D. H. Lawrence, and Henry Miller and is now legendary among bibliophiles—as is her bookstore.

Rizzoli (✉ 31 W. 57th St., ☎ 212/759–2424; ✉ 454 W. Broadway, near Prince St., ☎ 212/674–1616; ✉ World Financial Center, ☎ 212/385–1400). Uptown, an elegant marble entrance, oak paneling, chandeliers, and classical music accompany books and magazines on art, architecture, dance, design, photography, and travel; the downtown stores come with fewer frills.

Strand (✉ 828 Broadway, at 12th St., ☎ 212/473–1452; ✉ 95 Fulton St., ☎ 212/732–6070). The Broadway branch proudly claims to have 8 mi of books; craning your neck among the tall-as-trees stacks will likely net you something. The Fulton Street branch is close to South Street Seaport.

Cameras and Electronics

SONY Style (✉ 550 Madison Ave., between 55th and 56th Sts., ☎ 212/833–8800). Audio and video equipment comes in a glossy package here; plunge into the blue-velvet-swathed downstairs area for a demonstration.

CDs, Tapes, and Records

Bleecker Bob's Golden Oldies (✉ 118 W. 3rd St., ☎ 212/475–9677). The staff sells punk, new wave, progressive rock, and reggae, plus good old rock on vinyl, until the wee hours.

Footlight Records (✉ 113 E. 12th St., ☎ 212/533–1572). Stop here to browse through New York's largest selection of old and new musicals and movie soundtracks, as well as a good choice of jazz and popular recordings.

Gryphon Record Shop (✉ 251 W. 72nd St., 2nd floor, ☎ 212/874–1588). One of the city's best rare-record stores, it stocks some 90,000 out-of-print and rare LPs.

Tower Records and Videos (✉ 692 Broadway, at 4th St., ☎ 212/505–1500; ✉ 1961 Broadway, at 66th St., ☎ 212/799–2500; ✉ 725 5th Ave., basement level of Trump Tower, ☎ 212/838–8110). The selection of CDs and tapes can get overwhelming here.

Virgin Megastore Times Square (⊠ 1540 Broadway, between 45th and 46th Sts., ☎ 212/921–1020). Touted as the largest music-entertainment complex in the world, this glitzy emporium will impress you or give you a headache, depending on your mood.

Children's Clothing

Space Kiddets (⊠ 46 E. 21st St., ☎ 212/420–9878). Casual trendsetting clothes for kids are carried here.

Crystal

Baccarat (⊠ 625 Madison Ave., between 58th and 59th Sts., ☎ 212/826–4100) "Life is worth Baccarat," say the ads—in other words, the quality of crystal shown here is priceless.

Galleri Orrefors Kosta Boda (⊠ 58 E. 57th St., ☎ 212/752–1095). Stop here for striking Swedish crystal, including work from the imaginative and often brightly colored Kosta Boda line.

Steuben (⊠ 717 5th Ave., at 56th St., ☎ 212/752–1441). The stunning and adventurous designs on display often go beyond the basic vase.

Food

Balducci's (⊠ 424 6th Ave., at 9th St., ☎ 212/673–2600). In one of the city's finest food stores, mounds of baby carrots keep company with frilly lettuce, feathery dill, and superlative cheeses, chocolates, baked goods, pastas, vinegars, oils, and Italian specialties.

Kam-Man (⊠ 200 Canal St., ☎ 212/571–0330). The city's premier Chinese market, Kam-Man is filled with exotic foods, the staccato sound of Chinese, and mysterious smells.

Zabar's (⊠ 2245 Broadway, at 80th St., ☎ 212/787–2000). This is undoubtedly one of New York's favorite food markets. Dried herbs and spices, chocolates, and assorted bottled foods coexist with a fragrant jumble of fresh breads and the cheese, meat, and smoked-fish counters. Upstairs is a large selection of kitchenware.

Fragrance Shops

Aveda Environmental Lifestyle Store (⊠ 140 5th Ave., at 19th St., ☎ 212/645–4797). Concoct your own perfumes from the impressive selection of essential oils.

Floris (✉ 703 Madison Ave., between 62nd and 63rd Sts., ☎ 212/935–9100). Floral English toiletries beloved of such beauties as Cher and Catherine Deneuve fill this recreation of the cozy London original.

Home Decor and Gifts

Felissimo (✉ 10 W. 56th St., ☎ 212/247–5656). Spread over four stories of a Beaux Arts town house are unusual items, many handcrafted, that reconcile classic European and modern Asian sensibilities.

Moss (✉ 146 Greene St., ☎ 212/226–2190). This sleek boutique is decidedly contemporary, putting a fantastic spin on even the most utilitarian objects.

Jewelry, Watches, and Silver

Fortunoff (✉ 681 5th Ave., between 53rd and 54th Sts., ☎ 212/758–6660). Good prices on gold and silver jewelry, flatware, and hollow-ware draw crowds to this large store.

James Robinson (✉ 480 Park Ave., at 58th St., ☎ 212/752–6166). This family-owned business sells handmade flatware, antique silver, fine estate jewelry, and 18th- and 19th-century china.

Luggage and Leather Goods

Crouch & Fitzgerald (✉ 400 Madison Ave., at 48th St., ☎ 212/755–5888). Since 1839, this store has offered a terrific selection of hard- and soft-sided luggage, as well as handbags.

T. Anthony (✉ 445 Park Ave., at 56th St., ☎ 212/750–9797). This store's hard- and soft-sided luggage of coated fabric with leather trim has brass fasteners that look like precision machines.

Men's Clothing

Façonnable (✉ 689 5th Ave., at 54th St., ☎ 212/319–0111). Designed in France, the well-made traditional clothing and sportswear have an international appeal.

Paul Smith (✉ 108 5th Ave., at 16th St., ☎ 212/627–9770). Dark mahogany Victorian cases display downtown styles.

Paul Stuart Inc. (✉ Madison Ave. at 45th St., ☎ 212/682–0320). The fabric selection is interesting, the tailoring superb, and the look traditional but not stodgy.

Church's English Shoes (✉ 428 Madison Ave., at 49th St., ☎ 212/755–4313). This store has been selling beautifully made English shoes since 1873.

John Fluevog Shoes (✉ 104 Prince St., ☎ 212/431–4484). The inventor of the Angelic sole (protects against water, acid . . . and Satan), Fluevog designs chunky shoes and boots that are much more than mere Doc Marten copies.

Men's and Women's Clothing

Calvin Klein (✉ 654 Madison Ave., at 60th St., ☎ 212/292–9000). This huge, stark store showcases Calvin Klein's latest design collection.

Dolce & Gabbana (✉ 825 Madison Ave., between 68th and 69th Sts., no phone at press time). It's easy to feel like an Italian movie star in this two-level store (opened in fall 1997), which features attractive men's and women's collections.

Gucci (✉ 685 5th Ave., at 54th St., ☎ 212/826–2600). Designer Tom Ford's revamp campaign shows no signs of slowing down—the venerable name has an increasingly svelte edge.

Hermès (✉ 11 E. 57th St., ☎ 212/751–3181). Patterned silk scarves, neckties, and the sacred "Kelly" handbags are hallmarks.

Prada (✉ 841 Madison Ave., at 70th St., ☎ 212/327–4200). The interior pulses with pale "verdolino" green walls and lighting. The '60s-inspired clothes have proved to be another major Italian fashion coup—even the shoes and leather goods have become international status symbols. A smaller boutique is located at 45 East 57th Street.

Toys

Disney Store (✉ 711 5th Ave., ☎ 212/702–0702; ✉ 210 W. 42nd St., at 7th Ave., ☎ 212/221–0430; ✉ 39 W. 34th St., ☎ 212/279–9890; ✉ 147 Columbus Ave., at W. 66th St., ☎ 212/362–2386). All branches carry merchandise relating to Disney films and characters.

Enchanted Forest (✉ 85 Mercer St., between Spring and Broome Sts., ☎ 212/925–6677). There's all manner of curiosity-provoking gizmos, plus old-fashioned tin toys and a small but choice selection of children's books.

F.A.O. Schwarz (✉ 767 5th Ave., at 58th St., ☎ 212/644–9400). Beyond a wonderful mechanical clock with many dials and dingbats are tons of stuffed animals, dolls (including an inordinate number of Barbies), things to build with (including blocks by the pound), computer games, and much, much more.

Geppetto's Toy Box (✉ 161 7th Ave. S, between Perry and Charles Sts., ☎ 212/620–7511). Most toys here are handmade, ranging from extravagant costumed dolls to tried-and-true rubber duckies.

Women's Clothing

CLASSICS

Ann Taylor (✉ 2015–2017 Broadway, near 69th St., ☎ 212/873–7344; ✉ 2380 Broadway, at 87th St., ☎ 212/721–3130; ✉ 4 Fulton St., ☎ 212/480–4100; ✉ 645 Madison Ave., at 60th St., ☎ 212/832–2010; and other locations). This chain has nearly cornered the market for moderately priced, office-appropriate clothing and shoes.

Burberrys (✉ 9 E. 57th St., ☎ 212/371–5010). The look is classic and conservative, especially in the Burberrys signature plaid—and nobody does a better trench coat.

DESIGNER SHOWCASES

Chanel (✉ 15 E. 57th St., ☎ 212/355–5050). The flagship Chanel store, opened in 1996, has often been compared to a classic Chanel suit—slim, elegant, and timeless.

Christian Dior (✉ 703 5th Ave., at 55th St., ☎ 212/223–4646). Both daytime and evening clothes are offered, plus all the accessories (and scents) to enhance them.

Comme des Garçons (✉ 116 Wooster St., between Prince and Spring Sts., ☎ 212/219–0660). This SoHo shop showcases Japanese designer Rei Kawakubo.

Moschino (✉ 803 Madison Ave., between 67th and 68th Sts., ☎ 212/639–9600). People with a penchant for comedic couture won't have any trouble finding their wardrobe soul mate in this whirligig store.

Nicole Miller (✉ 780 Madison Ave., between 66th and 67th Sts., ☎ 212/288–9779; ✉ 134 Prince St., ☎ 212/343–1362). Known for her silk prints spoofing almost any topic imaginable (French wine, Dalmatians, dentistry), Nicole Miller also sells some simple dresses.

Todd Oldham (✉ 123 Wooster St., near Prince St., ☎ 212/219–3531). The cutting-edge designer's SoHo shop is the perfect antidote to too much beige.

Vera Wang (✉ 991 Madison Ave., at 77th St., ☎ 212/628–3400). Sumptuous, made-to-order bridal and evening wear is shown here by appointment only. Periodic prêt-à-porter sales offer designer dresses for a (relative) song.

Yves Saint Laurent Rive Gauche (✉ 855 Madison Ave., between 70th and 71st Sts., ☎ 212/988–3821). The looks range from chic to classic for day and evening. The men's boutique is right next door, at 859 Madison.

DISCOUNT

Century 21 (✉ 22 Cortlandt St., between Broadway and Church St., ☎ 212/227–9092; ✉ 472 86th St., Bay Ridge, Brooklyn, ☎ 718/748–3266). Spiffy quarters make bargain-hunting a pleasure, and there are fabulous buys on very high fashion.

HIP STYLES

Anna Sui (✉ 113 Greene St., between Prince and Spring Sts., ☎ 212/941–8406). The violet-and-black salon, hung with Beardsley prints and neon alterna-rock posters, is the perfect setting for Sui's flapper- and gangster-influenced designs.

Canal Jean (✉ 504 Broadway, between Spring and Broome Sts., ☎ 212/226–1130). Casual funk draws hip shoppers.

Charivari (✉ 257 Columbus Ave., at 72nd St., ☎ 212/787–7272; Charivari 57, ✉ 18 W. 57th St., ☎ 212/333–4040). Founder Selma Weiser has made a name for herself internationally for her eagle eye on the up-and-coming and avant-garde.

Miu Miu (⊠ 100 Prince St., ☎ 212/334–5156). Responding to the huge appetite for the designs of Miuccia Prada, the company opened its first North American Miu Miu boutique here. You can get the same straight-edged look for a little less money.

Trash and Vaudeville (⊠ 4 St. Mark's Pl., ☎ 212/982–3590). Black, white, and electric colors are the focus here—and you never know when you might see Lou Reed buying jeans.

VINTAGE

The 1909 Company (⊠ 63 Thompson St., between Spring and Broome Sts., ☎ 212/343–1658). A special display case holds the Gucci and Pucci, while the racks have classy '60s suits, all in great condition.

Screaming Mimi's (⊠ 382 Lafayette St., between 4th and Great Jones Sts., ☎ 212/677–6464). Vintage '60s and '70s clothes and retro-wear include everything from lingerie to prom dresses.

Women's Shoes

Hélène Arpels (⊠ 470 Park Ave., between 57th and 58th Sts., ☎ 212/755–1623). This is the grande dame of fine footwear for the well heeled.

Joan & David (⊠ 816 Madison Ave., at 68th St., ☎ 212/772–3970; ⊠ 104 5th Ave., at 16th St., ☎ 212/627–1780) can always be relied on for classy flats.

Peter Fox (⊠ 105 Thompson St., between Prince and Spring Sts., ☎ 212/431–7426; ⊠ 806 Madison Ave., between 67th and 68th Sts., ☎ 212/744–8340). Looks here are outside the fashion mainstream—really fun.

Flea Markets

Annex Antiques Fair and Flea Market (⊠ 6th Ave. at 26th St., ☎ 212/243–5343). Weekends year-round.

INDEX

X = restaurant, ▥ = hotel

NOTES

NOTES

NOTES

Fodor's Travel Publications

Available at bookstores everywhere, or call 1–800–533–6478, 24 hours a day.

Gold Guides

U.S.

Alaska

Arizona

Boston

California

Cape Cod, Martha's Vineyard, Nantucket

The Carolinas & Georgia

Chicago

Colorado

Florida

Hawai'i

Las Vegas, Reno, Tahoe

Los Angeles

Maine, Vermont, New Hampshire

Maui & Lāna'i

Miami & the Keys

New England

New Orleans

New York City

Pacific North Coast

Philadelphia & the Pennsylvania Dutch Country

The Rockies

San Diego

San Francisco

Santa Fe, Taos, Albuquerque

Seattle & Vancouver

The South

U.S. & British Virgin Islands

USA

Virginia & Maryland

Walt Disney World, Universal Studios and Orlando

Washington, D.C.

Foreign

Australia

Austria

The Bahamas

Belize & Guatemala

Bermuda

Canada

Cancún, Cozumel, Yucatán Peninsula

Caribbean

China

Costa Rica

Cuba

The Czech Republic & Slovakia

Eastern & Central Europe

Europe

Florence, Tuscany & Umbria

France

Germany

Great Britain

Greece

Hong Kong

India

Ireland

Israel

Italy

Japan

London

Madrid & Barcelona

Mexico

Montréal & Québec City

Moscow, St. Petersburg, Kiev

The Netherlands, Belgium & Luxembourg

New Zealand

Norway

Nova Scotia, New Brunswick, Prince Edward Island

Paris

Portugal

Provence & the Riviera

Scandinavia

Scotland

Singapore

South Africa

South America

Southeast Asia

Spain

Sweden

Switzerland

Thailand

Toronto

Turkey

Vienna & the Danube Valley

Special-Interest Guides

Adventures to Imagine

Alaska Ports of Call

Ballpark Vacations

Caribbean Ports of Call

The Complete Guide to America's National Parks

Disney Like a Pro

Europe Ports of Call

Family Adventures

Fodor's Gay Guide to the USA

Fodor's How to Pack

Great American Learning Vacations

Great American Sports & Adventure Vacations

Great American Vacations

Great American Vacations for Travelers with Disabilities

Halliday's New Orleans Food Explorer

Healthy Escapes

Kodak Guide to Shooting Great Travel Pictures

National Parks and Seashores of the East

National Parks of the West

Nights to Imagine

Rock & Roll Traveler Great Britain and Ireland

Rock & Roll Traveler USA

Sunday in San Francisco

Walt Disney World for Adults

Weekends in New York

Wendy Perrin's Secrets Every Smart Traveler Should Know

Where Should We Take the Kids? California

Where Should We Take the Kids? Northeast

Worldwide Cruises and Ports of Call

Fodor's Special Series

Fodor's Best Bed & Breakfasts

America

California

The Mid-Atlantic

New England

The Pacific Northwest

The South

The Southwest

The Upper Great Lakes

Compass American Guides

Alaska

Arizona

Boston

Chicago

Colorado

Hawai'i

Hollywood

Idaho

Las Vegas

Maine

Manhattan

Minnesota

Montana

New Mexico

New Orleans

Oregon

Pacific Northwest

San Francisco

Santa Fe

South Carolina

South Dakota

Southwest

Texas

Utah

Virginia

Washington

Wine Country

Wisconsin

Wyoming

Citypacks

Amsterdam

Atlanta

Berlin

Chicago

Florence

Hong Kong

London

Los Angeles

Montréal

New York City

Paris

Prague

Rome

San Francisco

Tokyo

Venice

Washington, D.C.

Exploring Guides

Australia

Boston & New England

Britain

California

Canada

Caribbean

China

Costa Rica

Egypt

Florence & Tuscany

Florida

France

Germany

Greek Islands

Hawaii

Ireland

Israel

Italy

Japan

London

Mexico

Moscow & St. Petersburg

New York City

Paris

Prague

Provence

Rome

San Francisco

Scotland

Singapore & Malaysia

South Africa

Spain

Thailand

Turkey

Venice

Flashmaps

Boston

New York

San Francisco

Washington, D.C.

Fodor's Gay Guides

Los Angeles & Southern California

New York City

Pacific Northwest

San Francisco and the Bay Area

South Florida

USA

Pocket Guides

Acapulco

Aruba

Atlanta

Barbados

Budapest

Jamaica

London

New York City

Paris

Prague

Puerto Rico

Rome

San Francisco

Washington, D.C.

Languages for Travelers (Cassette & Phrasebook)

French

German

Italian

Spanish

Mobil Travel Guides

America's Best Hotels & Restaurants

California and the West

Great Lakes

Major Cities

Mid-Atlantic

Northeast

Northwest and Great Plains

Southeast

Southwest and South Central

Rivages Guides

Bed and Breakfasts of Character and Charm in France

Hotels and Country Inns of Character and Charm in France

Hotels and Country Inns of Character and Charm in Italy

Hotels and Country Inns of Character and Charm in Paris

Hotels and Country Inns of Character and Charm in Portugal

Hotels and Country Inns of Character and Charm in Spain

Short Escapes

Britain

France

Near New York City

New England

Fodor's Sports

Golf Digest's Places to Play

Skiing USA

USA Today The Complete Four Sport Stadium Guide

WHEREVER
YOU TRAVEL,
*H*ELP IS NEVER
FAR AWAY.

From planning your trip to providing travel assistance
along the way, American Express® Travel Service Offices
are always there to help you do more.

New York City

American Express Travel Service
New York Hilton Hotel
1335 Sixth Avenue
212/664-7798

American Express Travel Service
150 East 42nd Street
212/687-3700

American Express Travel Service
New York Marriott Marquis Hotel
1535 Broadway
212/575-6580

American Express Travel Service
American Express Tower
200 Vesey Street
212/640-5130

American Express Travel Service
200 Fifth Avenue
212/691-9797

American Express Travel Service
374 Park Avenue
212/421-8240

American Express Travel Service
JFK International Airport
Main Lobby
718/656-5673

do more AMERICAN EXPRESS

Travel

http://www.americanexpress.com/travel

American Express Travel Service Offices are located throughout
New York City. For the office nearest you, call 1-800-AXP-3429.

Listings are valid as of May 1997. Not all services available at all locations.
©1997 American Express Travel Related Services Company, Inc.